70 Years of Reaching Fo
Shaw Cross Rugby Leag

Graham Williams

London League Publications Ltd

70 Years of Reaching Forward
Shaw Cross Rugby League Club

© Graham Williams. Foreword © Michael Stephenson.
The moral right of Graham Williams to be identified as the author has been asserted.
Cover design © Stephen McCarthy.
Cover photos: Front: Andrew Fawkes enjoying summer rugby. Back: The Shaw Cross tots and 1949–50 team group in front of the Nissan Hut. The Shaw Cross crest and 70th Anniversary logo were both designed by Brett Turner.

A CIP catalogue record for this book is available from the British Library.

First published in Great Britain in October 2017 by London League Publications Ltd, PO Box 65784, London NW2 9NS

ISBN: 978-1-909885-14-1

Cover design by Stephen McCarthy Graphic Design
46, Clarence Road, London N15 5BB

Editing and layout by Peter Lush

Printed and bound in Great Britain by Ashford Colour Press Ltd, Gosport, Hants PO13 0FW

Foreword

It is with great pride and pleasure that our world famous club can celebrate such a momentous milestone in sporting history. We've come a long way since that day in 1947 when the decision was made to form a youth club and I thank all those concerned in the early years who overcame many obstacles to ensure they laid the foundations for what has become one of the leading sporting clubs of this country.

Obviously, a special mention must go to Dougie Hird, who had the vision to help set up an organisation that gave local youngsters the opportunity to indulge in sport at a time when the country was struggling to get back on its feet after the Second World War. Since that day sheer determination and hard work has ensured that the youngsters in Dewsbury and the surrounding areas are given the chance to embark on a satisfying and enjoyable participation of sport at its highest level.

Of course, such achievements could not have happened without the many coaches, players, managers, committee members, sponsors and those wonderful parents who have made many sacrifices to ensure the club continued to expand.

From that first year when the Second World War Nissan hut was erected, our club has expanded to now offer top class facilities to the youth of our area and we feel proud that we extend such a warm welcome to all those who walk through our door. Again, we thank all those people who have worked tirelessly to offer refreshments to our players, supporters and friends of all ages.

Over the years we've celebrated much glory as our teams have won many trophies and showed that our proud area can produce athletes of world-class performance and hundreds have gone on to secure professional careers at most of the rugby league clubs in this country. Some players have gone as far afield as France, Papua New Guinea, New Zealand and Australia to play both professional and amateur rugby league.

All this of course could not have been possible without setting such a high level of coaching and management standards. We thank all those who have left their mark throughout those years and also our present staff who I know will maintain them.

Not everyone has gone on to become a prominent player at the top level and whilst we are extremely satisfied at producing such talented high-profile individuals, we must never forget all those who helped make up the team, the hard workers who gave their all for their teammates both on and off the field of play. Without such dedication those who went on to bigger and better things would never have had the chance to make their mark. Most importantly, our club is proud to have offered youngsters the chance to change their lives and be guided to take the right road in life and avoid the many pitfalls that are offered in this hectic ever changing world.

Our club will continue to keep the door open to everyone and help give the young people of our community a chance to become one of sport's highest accolades – a 'Shaw Cross Member'.

Michael Stephenson MBE (Club President)

Introduction

2017 marks the 70th birthday of the Shaw Cross club. On the afternoon of Sunday 17 September 2017 the Shaw Cross Club for Young People celebrated its 70th birthday. That afternoon saw over 300 guests and a few of guests of honour assemble at the Cedar Court Hotel in Wakefield for the club's annual dinner. Those celebrations will mark an enormous achievement by a remarkable club which has grown from humble origins to become a force at the grassroots of rugby league. It is certainly worthy of celebration. It is testimony to the hard work and drive of those involved that the passion of a few youths would turn into a great club that is recognised as one of the great rugby league nurseries. Over those 70 years the club has achieved a huge amount and I hope in this book the reader will get some idea of the work that has been put in both on and off the field to make the club so well known in its home town and across the north of England.

While the first team – the Sharks – grabs much of the attention I hope this run through the years also captures something of the life of the whole club. Because it is important to remember that while the club may be most famous for the number of players it has prepared for a professional career its greatest achievement is perhaps the thousands of youngsters who have learned to love rugby league in its junior teams over the years.

Putting together this anniversary tribute to the club has been a very interesting challenge. It would not have been possible without lots of help and I have been fortunate to have the support of those involved in running the club and would particularly like to thank Douglas Hird, Chris Smith, Mick Turner, Alan Smith and Nigel Walsh for the time they have made available in the preparation of this history. There was also much appreciated assistance from the staff at the Leeds City reference library.

Once again, thanks go to Peter Lush and Dave Farrar at London League Publications Ltd for seeing the project through from the start to final publication.

Graham Williams

Graham Williams has been following rugby league for nearly 50 years. A Leeds Rhinos fan, he developed an interest in the history of the game and from that began writing about it. Over the years he has had articles published in *Open Rugby, Code 13, Our Game, Rugby League Journal* and *Rugby League Review Number 2*.

In addition to articles he also authored or co-authored a number of books. Those on rugby league have included *Rugby's Berlin Wall*, the biographies of Peter Fox and Mick Sullivan and the *British Rugby League Records Book*.

Thank you

Thank you to everyone at Shaw Cross who contributed to this book, to Graham Williams for writing it, everyone who supplied photographs, Steve McCarthy for designing the cover and the staff at Ashford Colour Press Ltd for printing the book.

Peter Lush and Dave Farrar
London League Publications Ltd

Contents

1. Early days at Shaw Cross

Beyond Crown Flatt and Mount Pleasant, where Dewsbury and Batley had hosted War Emergency League matches throughout the conflict, very little Rugby League had been played in the district except in a few schools such as St Paulinus (the future St John Fisher) and Earlsheaton Secondary. Peace brought with it the need to resurrect the junior game in Dewsbury and Batley.

Before the war the district had been made famous for the exploits of the Dewsbury boys' team and later for the successes of the Dewsbury Black Knights, an under-18 team formed by Eddie Waring. Nobody doubted that the talent which had powered those pre-war youth teams was still there and that provided the inspiration for those keen to get the game going again.

Shaw Cross, which lies on the Leeds Road about a mile-and-a-half north of Dewsbury town centre, was then little more than a pit village lying in the shadow of two local collieries. Today the site of the larger of those two collieries on Owl Lane is the better known as the Ram Stadium. It was a fairly typical pit village with a few local amenities – a post office, a grocers, two fish and chip shops – serving its 2,000 inhabitants.

The Shaw Cross Boys Club as it was then known, burst into life in 1947. Although many things were in short supply in post-war Britain, there was no shortage of enthusiasm among a group of lads in Shaw Cross.

Douglas Hird, who was one of that group of determined lads, described the formation of the club in *40 years and more of Reaching Forward*. As Douglas remembered it all started when "A number of teenage of boys, of which I was one, decided to form a club of their own so that they could play rugby league football. We were about a dozen, all living in and around Shaw Cross, most of us had gone to school together and were then attending evening classes at Dewsbury and Batley Technical and Art College. The idea to start the club really came one night as we trudged up the steep Halifax Road to the Tech. We discussed all manner of things on these treks and somehow we were determined to do something at Shaw Cross – it was a sort of challenge – and we decided to give it a go.

There was nothing at Shaw Cross, no youth club and nowhere to go. Our early youth had been spent in somewhat austere days during the Second World War with long periods of restrictions and rationing when quite naturally the nation's effort had been geared to winning the war. Instead of doing maths we had been knitting squares to make blankets for the troops or fastening buttons on Army denim jackets.

But then the war was over and everyone was looking to the future. There was just the old recreation ground at Shaw Cross but even the swings, the slide and the monkey-climb on which we had played so much in our younger days were now derelict and indeed, some of the parts and pieces had been removed for the war effort. The underground air-raid shelters still remained in the recreation ground but even so, we visualised a rugby pitch in the middle.

We decided to form a team, to be called 'Shaw Cross'. Odds were against us because at that time there were several well established and strong sides in the town, including Dewsbury YMCA which ran three teams. It was with some reluctance that I agreed to be secretary because I knew nothing about running a rugby team, my only aptitude being a little shorthand and typing. Among the founder members were Gordon Waring, who had persuaded me to act as secretary, Eric Bailey, Desmond Reynolds, John Fisher, Sam Waterhouse, Stan Talbot, Harold Fortis and others. An approach was made to the late Harry V. Smith, then secretary of the Dewsbury and Batley Amateur Rugby League, who became a close friend to us all.

We had no money, no premises and no pitch — what we had in great measure was perhaps the most important thing — enthusiasm. Each of us subscribed half a crown and we acquired a set of green and black jerseys from the Dewsbury and Batley Amateur Rugby League. Mr Smith soon arranged some fixtures for us and for a time, because we had no ground, we played all our matches away from home.

Our first game was at Healey, Batley, and we began with a defeat, 11–0. Actually on that first day we turned out with only 11 players as the Healey officials objected to two of our members, Eric Bailey and Desmond Reynolds, alleging they were over age. It was then an under–18 league. On later producing their birth certificates these two players were found to be eligible and played for us in future games.

Throughout this time our own pitch was taking shape in the recreation ground at Shaw Cross. Dewsbury Corporation had given us permission to use the ground, but much preparatory work was necessary. The concrete bases of the monkey-climb and slide required digging-up and removing, as did many stones from the adjacent derelict air-raid shelters. Fortunately at this time work was taking place on the new Leeds Road between Shaw Cross and Chidswell and the foreman kindly allowed us to borrow picks, wheelbarrows and shovels at weekends and during the evenings. Our pitch was soon ready and although full-length was rather narrow. As Gordon Waring was an apprentice joiner in Shaw Cross we were never short of sawdust for the field markings.

For several months we had no premises at all and the club actually functioned in the open air, meetings being informal on the field after a game; and in the first match at Shaw Cross, both teams had to strip behind a wall and afterwards wash from a bucket of cold water. From this we graduated in turn to a garage, a greenhouse, a garden hut, one of the boy's own houses, and the Chidswell Mount Tabor Chapel Schoolroom.

There were no luxury coaches to transport the team to away games. However, whatever else we lacked, it wasn't good connections, and as in those days the Talbot family was in business as coal merchant, one of the founder boys, Stan Talbot would often turn up with a coal lorry and the players would be delivered at away grounds with half a ton of best nuts! Things were certainly different in those days and somewhat primitive, but the spirit and enthusiasm of the members soon began to attract others.

Stanley Waring, whose son Gordon was a founder member, was persuaded to help and was appointed the first club leader. One of the greatest difficulties was to keep the club out of the 'red' and a very careful eye had to be kept on all expenditure. However, we were determined to have our own premises as soon as possible, and eventually by various efforts, we had saved enough money to buy a club house of our own – an old Nissen hut which we acquired for the enormous sum of £30.

We had to fetch the Nissen hut from a former military camp site between Wakefield and Doncaster where the hut lay dismantled looking nothing more than a pile of old iron in a field. The late Mr Jack Dawson, another adult helper, joined us about this time and assisted in bringing the iron jigsaw puzzle back to Shaw Cross. We didn't realise it then, fortunately perhaps, what a difficult job it was going to be to put it all together again.

Dewsbury Corporation had given us the necessary permission to erect the hut in the old recreation ground adjoining our pitch and for several weeks during evenings and weekend it was a case of everyone rolling up their sleeves and helping. However, despite many setbacks, our enthusiasm never waned and eventually in the summer of 1949 our club house was completed.

It was a great day when Alderman RS Roberts, whom we shortly afterwards asked to become our president, officially opened the club house. A number of bus seats had been acquired and fitted down the sides of the hut interior, there was an old combination stove in the middle and we even had curtains at the windows provided by our first ladies committee, mainly comprising boys' mothers. Incidentally these ladies in those early and difficult days, provided us with a cup of tea, and a sandwich after home games and thus laid the foundation of the wonderful co-operation and support which the club has enjoyed from its ladies committee ever since.

Opening day was marked by playing and defeating Dewsbury YMCA Wanderers at Shaw Cross. The YMCA were then the strongest team in the league and it was a wonderful triumph for Shaw Cross to celebrate the club opening ceremony with a 10–5 victory."

While so much of importance was going on away from the pitch, the boys were making a name for themselves on it. As Douglas mentioned above, the club had joined the Dewsbury and Batley Amateur Rugby League which ran competitions at under–18 and under–16 level. Both were strong competitions; the former regularly containing 10 teams spread across the twin towns while the latter often included half-a-dozen. In its initial season the club ran two under–16 teams, an under–18 in the local competitions and an under–21 on occasion.

It took only three seasons for all that enthusiasm to be harnessed to bring home the first silverware – the under–18 team, under the captaincy of Jack Bye, won the Dewsbury and Batley ARL Championship.

Having made its mark on the twin towns, Shaw Cross set out to make the County take notice. By the end of the season, the Shaw Cross Boys' Club team had won through to play in the Yorkshire Under–21 final. Although it was an under–21 match, Mick Sullivan was only 16 and there were concerns for his safety in much older company, but he was so fast and so strong that it was decided he could not really be left out. He was picked and travelled with the team over to York to play the York based Imperial Athletic on Saturday 14 April. It was the Shaw Cross club's first appearance in a major County final and appearing alongside Mick Sullivan was another future test regular, Derek Turner, and five other players – Peter Blackburn (Dewsbury), Alan Lancaster (Bradford Northern, Huddersfield, Doncaster), Allen Lockwood (Dewsbury, Hull KR, Leeds), Peter Oldroyd (Rochdale Hornets) and Norman Wainwright (Huddersfield, Batley) – who went on to play professionally. The match did not go to plan for the visitors. Norman Wainwright, the captain, and Allen Lockwood were both dismissed and 'Pinky' Smith suffered a broken ankle. Short of three players, Shaw Cross did well to only lose 12–3.

Not long after joining Huddersfield Mick Sullivan brought reflected glory onto Shaw Cross by becoming the first of its products to gain national recognition when he was chosen to play for the England amateur team against France in February 1952. He backed up that performance by going to play for the England under–21 team in France two months later.

National Service

To cope with the onset of the Cold War and retreat from Empire, an increased military presence was needed and the Labour Government reluctantly agreed in May 1947 to retain conscription. Legislation was passed requiring all the country's young men to spend time serving His Majesty. National Service, as it was known, started on 1 January 1949 for young men between the ages of 18 and 26. Initially, it was for 18 months, but this increased to two years once the Korean War began in 1950.

There were exemptions for young miners if they wanted. The only other option a conscript had was to apply to defer his enlistment until he was older if he had a good reason, such as following an apprenticeship or attending university. Most chose to join up at 18 and get it over and done with. The vast majority found themselves directed to the Army, the rest going almost totally to the RAF because the Royal Navy chose not to become too reliant on conscripts.

A changing perception of the external threat and growing unpopularity at home after the Suez debacle in 1956 led to National Service being scaled down from the late 1950s onwards. Numbers fell as deferments increased until finally the call-up was ended at the start of 1961, what remained of that last intake were demobbed in May 1963. After that, the Army returned to being a regulars only outfit.

1949 Shaw Cross Under–18s: Back: E. Sugden, Dougie Hird, C. Gledhill, J. Donnelly, A. Frost, J. Bye, J. Fisher, J. Messenger, R. Smith, S. Beaumont, David Hird, D. Almond, S. Waring (Club Leader); front: M. Waring, R. Sugden, L. Peirson, G. Waring, E. Lodge, P. Messenger, A. Lancaster.

1949 Shaw Cross Under–16s Heavy Woollen Cup winners.

Shaw Cross 1953 Under–18s Reporter Cup winners: Back: D. Hird (Secretary), J. Farrar, M. Waring, B. Wilkinson, E. Wilson, D. Peace, F. Smith (Chairman), Front: D. (Ginger) Smith, D. Smith, D. Moorhouse, H. Waring, A. Kilroy, J. Smith, G. Bradshaw, C. Towler.

Norman Wainwright and Mick Sullivan wearing their NABC rugby union caps.
(Courtesy Michelle Sullivan)

National Service lasted nearly 14 years and most of Shaw Cross's members served, many overseas. Once abroad most could only play occasionally while on leave. Others who were posted nearer home, played fairly regularly and for their service sides, albeit at rugby union, because league was not played in the Armed Forces at this time. Despite all this during National Service, the club continued to prosper.

Drawing once again on Douglas Hird's memories, how the club obtained another hut can be told: "In 1953 the club expanded its premises by obtaining another hut – the "top" hut – wooden and corrugated iron building, shown above. This was bought for the sum of £200 and had to be dismantled and transported from Morecambe. Under the leadership of Harry Waring (the brother of Eddie), two weekend trips were made to the West Coast, members travelling in Mr Waring's vans, and the hut was dismantled, each part marked with paint and a plan of the hut drawn by Mr K.S. Archer to assist in re-erection. The hut was quickly erected at Shaw Cross and became very useful for the already overcrowded club. Our first function in the 'new hut' was the annual harvest festival on 11 October 1953 which was a colourful spectacle and great success. Afterwards we held weekly whist drives in the Top Hut as it became known, which were organised by the women's committee. We also acquired a new table tennis table and a dart board for the members."

Douglas Hird remembers the problems the club faced at the start of May 1956. Saturday 5 May saw the team playing away in a cup final. The team lost, but the day became memorable for other even sadder reasons: "Our Nissen hut headquarters, which 18 months previously had been supposedly strengthened with breeze block, collapsed resulting in a total wreck. A strong gale force wind across the valley had proved too much for the old Nissen hut. The end came suddenly and many hours of labour crashed into a heap of rubble within a few seconds. It was particularly fortunate the building was unoccupied at the time of collapse. It was enough to bring an end to the club, but again the spirit and determination of the Shaw Cross lads ensured its' rebuilding. This time we built it with brick and a wooden roof. It was a much more permanent and safer building. It cost us just over £200, which was a lot in those days. In order that Shaw Cross Junior School could be extended, additional land was taken which deprived us of half of our playing pitch at the side of the club and thus we were without a home ground. For the next two seasons our 'home' fixtures were played two miles away at the Sands Lane Ground and then new pitches became available at 'Clayponds' at Leeds Road."

The National Association of Boys' Clubs

When striving to create their club at Shaw Cross the lads could take heart from the fact that they were not alone. Although independent and proud of it, they drew support from the boys' club movement. Thanks to that wider influence the club for many years provided opportunities for boys to play other sports and take part in other cultural and educational activities. The National Association of Boys' Clubs (NABC) had been founded in October 1925 and through it and its county and district bodies inspired and assisted young start-ups like the one at Shaw Cross.

Part of that inspiration was a steady stream of invites to take part in activities sponsored by the NABC. In many cases Shaw Cross did not actually organise its members around those activities, but likely candidates were encouraged to volunteer. Their names went forward and quite a number achieved success in various events at county level in the athletics, swimming and other competitions.

It was through this route that the club received invites to nominate some of its young rugby players for possible selection for the NABC's England versus Wales rugby union internationals. These were held annually and although the club had no involvement with rugby union, seven Shaw Cross boys represented the English clubs.
1950–51: Norman Wainwright and Mike Sullivan
1951–52: David V. Smith, Mike Sullivan and Austin Kilroy
1952–53: Austin Kilroy, David 'Ginger' Smith and Harry Waring
1953–54: David 'Ginger' Smith and Harry Waring

After 1954, rugby union invitations forwarded by the Yorkshire Association dried up. This appears to have been specific to Yorkshire because rugby league playing boys' clubs in other northern counties received invitations in the 1950s and have players selected. Shaw Cross was never again involved in NABC rugby union.

Locally the YABC organised its own cup competitions. Shaw Cross was a very successful entrant until the competitions lapsed in the 1960s. Then, invitations to support a YABC Rugby League team started to come and two boys – Robert Gowan and Peter Dransfield – went to the under–18 trials in 1967. They were followed by two more – John Frain and Brian Harrison – the following year.

By the start of the 1990s, changes were occurring in what had been the boys' club movement. Many clubs were no longer just boys. Girls had been taking an active part for some time and to recognise this the NABC changed its name to NABC – Clubs for Young People in 1992. Seven years later that changed to the National Association of Clubs for Young People. In 2005, the organisation's name became simply Clubs for Young People and then in 2012 just Ambition.

2. Growing pains

By the early 1960s, the club was facing a different set of challenges. A rapidly increasing membership meant that by 1963 it was clear that larger premises were needed. Douglas described what happened next in his 1968 history of the club, *21 years Reaching Forward:* "Under the guidance of Mr Bill Brazier, secretary of the Yorkshire Association of Boys' Clubs it was decided to form a development committee to raise the necessary funds. Prominent business and professional men in the town were invited to a dinner at Dewsbury Town Hall at which the chairman of National Association off Boys' Clubs, Viscount Althorp MVO – the future Earl Spencer and father of Princess Diana, travelled from London to launch an appeal.

Meetings were held at regular intervals and before long details of an £8,000 scheme were placed before the Ministry of Education. In due time the Ministry agreed to make a 50 per cent grant towards the cost and the Dewsbury Education Authority followed suit with a 25 per cent grant. The committee was then left with the task of raising the balance.

It seemed like a huge challenge at the time, but happily for the club, the target was achieved and on 20 March 1965 the new building was officially opened by the chairman of the appeal committee in the presence of a large company of distinguished guests and friends of the club."

Containing a main hall-gymnasium, fully equipped canteen, office and committee room, dressing and changing rooms, baths-showers, toilets, kit room, coaches', referees' and medical room the new building was an impressive facility. Later in the 1960s additional dressing and changing facilities were added.

21st birthday wishes

In 1968, the club decided to celebrate its 21st birthday. A book was produced and Eddie Waring contributed a foreword to it. By now he was one of the best known figures in rugby league, and was the BBC's television commentator. In it, Eddie said "My own personal interest in the Shaw Cross Boys' Club was always maintained because of keenness and enthusiastic support my late brother, Harry, gave to the club. He served as club leader and had much affection for the club until his death. He was very proud to be associated with the club, proud of its achievements in sport and pleased with its contribution of turning boys into men for Dewsbury."

Representative honours

At the start of 1960s there was not just quantity on show at Shaw Cross, there was plenty of quality too. It was not just the club officials who recognised that fact, the England under–19 selectors were soon showing they knew too. Trevor Bedford was called up to play full back against France in April 1961. Having signed for Castleford Trevor was chosen for England against France Under–24s in April 1965. In 1963 Kenneth Huxley also had the distinction of playing against France at Wakefield.

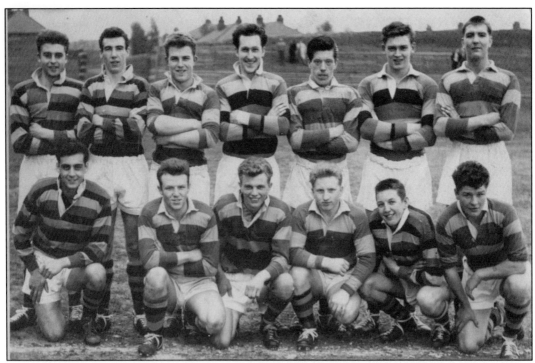

Shaw Cross Rovers 1960 Back: S. Jackson, K. Osborne, B. Taylor, S. Kelly, B. Walker, B. Hardcastle, D. Manners; front: M. Womack, A. Grayshon, A. Edwards, C. Page, D. Bradshaw, R. Wood.

Bernard Scott scoring a try for Shaw Cross against Westtown in the 1960 Reporter Cup Final at Dewsbury's Crown Flatt ground.

Presentation night at Dewsbury Town Hall in 1960.

Lord St. Oswald opening the new baths and showers in 1960.

Shaw Cross Wasps Under–17s 1965–66. Back: David O'Connor (Coach), D. Spencer, D. Thompson, C. Tidball, B. Judge, N. Stephenson, J. Frain, D. Senior, T. Lister; front: A. Haigh, D. North, R. Gomersall, D. Briggs. (Captain), B. Harrison, K. Kain, S. Lambert.

Shaw Cross Under–19s in the 1960s: Ian Sharpe, Billy Wood, Peter Lovell, Brian Armitage, David Judge, Ged Brentnall, Paul O'Hara, Peter Dransfield, Graham Pitchforth, Tony Hepworth, Bernard Walford, Jack Hemmins, Stephen Charlton, Paul Robinson, Peter Berry, David Senior, Graham Bell.

Indoor training in the late 1960s: Urek Piwinski, David Brooke, Ged Birkin, Mick Snee, Geoff Catlin and Colin Shires.

When Mick Sullivan returned from Australia he briefly coached Batley. Chairman Les Driver introduces him to new signings Steve Grinhaff, Urek Piwinski, Phil Taylor, David Brooke and Ged Birkin.

Shaw Cross Wasps 1961–62, one of the most successful sides in the club's history, coached by Jack Shaw. Back: J.Bell, D. Heppleston, G. Pearson, K. Huxley, B. Kendall, J. Sharp, A. Rider, J. Mitchell, P. Blackburn; front: A. Hayman, M. Connelly, G. Smith, D. Sanderson, M. Harris, M. Bedford, G. Marsh, T. Hobson, W. Calvert.

Then, in March 1965 the club excelled itself. Dewsbury supplied seven of the team that met France at Rochdale. Of those seven lads Shaw Cross supplied five, a national record. Those five were John Clark, vice-captain Tony Halmshaw, Michael Killbank, John Maloney and Darryl Woolin. The captain on the day was another Dewsbury lad, Bernard Watson, who in later years coached at Shaw Cross.

For John Maloney that marked the start of a memorable six months. He signed for Hull, and made his first team debut at the start of October. Less than three weeks later John played for the England under–24 team against France at Oldham. Playing alongside him was another Shaw Cross product, Brian Taylor. The under–24 matches were intended to be a pathway to the British team, but sadly neither Brian, John nor Trevor won full international honours. It did not prove possible to reach such heights again, but April 1969 saw Alan Bence packing down against France at Bradford. At the end of the following season David Redfearn appeared for the under–19s against France in Avignon. Two years later, David Redfearn, by now with Bradford Northern, gained a second under–19 cap alongside his former club mate Colin Shires when they played against France at Villeurbanne.

At this time the club was fielding seven rugby league teams each week and was considered to have the strongest teams in the district, regularly winning the League and Reporter cups at under–19 and the League and Boffin cups at under–17 levels.

Home help – Dewsbury's revival

The national selectors were not alone in taking an interest in Shaw Cross. Brearley Bailey had taken over as president of a cash strapped Dewsbury RLFC and embarked on a policy of building the town's professional team around local lads. Bailey not only kept a close watch on the talent coming in at Shaw Cross, but he was one of the most decisive. While he couldn't always match the money that was being paid to some of the leading juniors there was plenty more talent round he did manage to sign for his club. So persuasive was he that towards the end of 1964–65, Dewsbury took the field for a league match with 11 Shaw Cross products in the team.

Dewsbury had rarely come close to lifting any trophy since the late 1940s, but thanks largely to Bailey's signings the club underwent a revival and by the mid-1960s stood on the verge of returning to Wembley. A key part of that was the appointment of Shaw Cross legend, Mick Sullivan, to be captain–coach in September 1965.

Contrary to most expectations Dewsbury made it into the Challenge Cup semi-final, and a meeting with a strong St Helens team, led by Alex Murphy, at Swinton on Saturday 16 April 1966. The Dewsbury team, as the match programme pointed out, was not only local but also heavily reliant on Shaw Cross players. Six of the 15 named – Geoff Marsh, Kevin Osborne, Trevor Walker, Peter Mullins, Brian Taylor and Trevor Lowe – had been recruited direct from the club, while Alan Edwards was another Shaw Cross lad who had first turned professional with another club. Dewsbury's first peacetime semi-final appearance for 37 years was a titanic struggle. With Wembley Stadium only 80 minutes away, Dewsbury's team were certainly motivated. Facing a Saints' team who were probably over confident, Dewsbury took full advantage with an early 5–0 lead through an Alvyn Newall drop-goal and a Geoff Marsh try. Having gone ahead, Dewsbury defended doggedly.

It was a very physical clash that had plenty of incidents, none more so than when Minnie Cotton marched onto the pitch and tried to assault Trevor Walker with her umbrella for being too rough with her lodger, Saints' Welsh forward John Warlow. Despite losing stand-off Alan Edwards with a broken jaw, Dewsbury still led on the hour, before two Len Killeen tries saved the day for the Saints.

For two members of that team there was another highlight to come before the season ended. Peter Mullins and Brian Taylor were chosen to play for an RFL XIII that met a Paris XIII at the Parc des Princes at the start of May. Sadly, the trip did not produce a win, the British lads being thoroughly outclassed on the day.

Mick Sullivan left the club at the start of the following season, but his absence did not prevent Dewsbury making another huge effort to reach Wembley. Once more they reached the last four and again played their semi-final at Swinton. Barrow, their opponents, were also in a mid-table position and hopes were high of further progress. There was once again a half-dozen Shaw Cross lads in the team – Alan Edwards, Kevin Osborne, Geoff Marsh, Brian Taylor, Trevor Lowe and newcomer Jim Naylor. It could have been more but a young Mike Stephenson was dropped after playing in the quarter-final. Over 5,000 Dewsbury fans travelled to cheer on their team. At the break, Barrow led 8–7 but in the second-half Dewsbury could not quite break through and could only add a late Trevor Lowe penalty goal and lost 14–9.

Although he had by then stepped down, Brearley Bailey's policy continued to show its soundness when a new generation of Shaw Cross players made their mark at the club. By this time, Shaw Cross was almost seen as Dewsbury's nursery team, a relationship made to appear even stronger when they adopted the senior club's colours of red, amber and black.

Over 1972–73 Dewsbury made huge improvements, but it seemed their efforts would not be rewarded. The first chance of honours came at the start of October. Dewsbury had battled through to the final of the Yorkshire Cup for the first time since the Second World War. Missing Nigel Stephenson through injury, Dewsbury could not contain Leeds who proved far too strong winning 36–9 at Odsal. An early exit from the Player's Number 6 Trophy did not auger well, but Dewsbury' form was improving and the second half of the season surprised the rugby league world.

Six months after the disappointment of the Yorkshire Cup Final, Dewsbury returned to Headingley in the semi-final of the Challenge Cup. Many pundits rated their chances against a Bradford Northern side struggling for form in the league, but on the day the men from Odsal took control to win 33–14. Hopes seemed slim of Dewsbury gaining any further rewards as they began the Championship play-offs, having finished eighth in the League.

The play-offs featured the top 16 clubs that season and Dewsbury began with good, if not spectacular, wins over Oldham and Featherstone Rovers. Dewsbury's chances were re-appraised after a surprise win over Warrington, the league leaders, in the semi-final at Wilderspool. Dewsbury had reached the final, where Leeds awaited them at Odsal. Turning the form book on its head Dewsbury beat Leeds 22–13 to be crowned champions of the Northern Rugby League for the first time.

It was a proud day for the town and also for Shaw Cross which provided eight first-teamers that season – Grahame Bell, John Clark, Trevor Lowe, Brian Robinson, Mike Stephenson, Nigel Stephenson, Brian Taylor and Joe Whittington. By the end of the match, Nigel Stephenson had contributed 15 points, five goals and a try, to Dewsbury's total while his namesake Mike, Dewsbury's captain, added a further six points with two tries. For driving his team on to success, 'Stevo' was awarded the Harry Sunderland trophy as the man of the match.

That match was Stevo's last for the club. By the time the next season kicked off he had signed for Sydney's Penrith Panthers. His departure could have derailed the club, but again it picked itself up. While they did not retain the Championship, they mounted a strong campaign in the Challenge Cup which saw them reach the semi-final again. Wigan's Central Park was the venue for their match with Warrington. Dewsbury's days of mounting a serious challenge for the game's top honours were coming to a close as in tandem the number of Shaw Cross products in the team fell away. This time there were just four Shaw Cross products challenging for places in the first team – John Clark, the evergreen Trevor Lowe, Nigel Stephenson and John Maloney who had returned to the club after eight years with Hull. On the day, Alex Murphy's 'Wire' team, the eventual winners, proved too strong, winning 17–7.

It had been a remarkable decade for Dewsbury and Shaw Cross was proud to have played a central part in it.

3. Moving home

The times were certainly changing around Shaw Cross in the late 1960s. Coal mining ceased around the village and Leeds Road was widened. With the advent of the 1970s, major developments were planned which would expand the old village. Many new houses were to be built round about including a council estate.

To accommodate all these changes the club's old pitch, handily placed for the Nissen hut, was lost when the Council decided it was needed for the development of the Shaw Cross primary and infants school. A new home was needed and that was found on the Sands Lane fields by the River Calder in Dewsbury. Being two miles away from the club's facilities that was not a great location but help was on hand and two season later the club was able to move to the Bywell Road grounds which been developed by the Council. Finally, the club made it back home when the Council developed the Grange Road playing fields where the club now leases space for three pitches.

The Wembley trip

Throughout their history, Shaw Cross Sharks have usually organised trips to Wembley for the Rugby League Challenge Cup Final. When Douglas Hird was clearing out a cabinet recently he came across one of his old invoices from the National Bus Company for their Wembley outing in 1973.

To hire of one 49-seater coach Dewsbury to Wembley and return
£70.00: less 5% commission £3.50   £66.50
Also 50 tickets at £1.59 each
Plus VAT £8.00   £87.50

                                                    £154. 00
                                                    ======

Nowadays a coach to Wembley, returning the same day costs at least £1,000 and the cost of tickets for the match £60 or £70 each. How costs have risen.

A time of major upheavals

At the end of the 1960s, the Dewsbury and Batley District League was renamed the Heavy Woollen ARL. It was not a name change that enlivened the old organisation, which although it had a strong Sunday league, was reduced at the start of 1973–74 to just four under–19 and one under–17 members. Shaw Cross was the only club to be found in membership of both age groups. The twin towns were no different to many other parts of rugby league's heartland, which at the start of the 1970s, saw the game in serious decline.

Shaw Cross Hornets Under–17s Yorkshire Cup winners versus Hull in 1970. Back: Eric Hampshire (Coach) Brian Field, Stuart Broadhead, Stev Brown, Mick Basten, Dave Mordue, Howard Evans, Steve Halloran, Mick Snee, Steve Booth; front: Colin Hampshire, Colin Shires, David Ward (Capt) Geoff Catlin, Jimmy Campbell, David Smith, Jeff Crawshaw. Absent: Dean Wilson.

David Ward pulls the first pint in the old club house.

1973–74 Presentation night with League Champions Dewsbury.

It fell to a group of amateur officials in nearby Huddersfield to try and put the amateur game back on its feet. A meeting was called on Saturday 4 March 1973 at the Greenside Working Men's Club in Moldgreen, Huddersfield. After a good debate, a packed meeting agreed to break away from the RFL and form a separate British Amateur Rugby League Association (BARLA). This was not appreciated by the RFL which placed the new 'outlaw' organisation out of bounds.

Whatever the breakaway association's status, its forward plan published by Tom Keaveney, the secretary, at the end of June had much to commend them, particularly this section: "The top priority, as stated in our development plan is, logically, to plan for the future, and this means capturing 18-year-old youths now and so ensuring a reservoir of talent for tomorrow. The success of all good building and healthy growth is, as always, from the bottom and not from the top". It was an approach that dovetailed with the Shaw Cross way.

Initially, the RFL took a very hard line against the upstart organisation, but slowly over the next 12 months attitudes mellowed. In March 1974 the RFL unanimously agreed to back BARLA and full control of the amateur game was ceded to the new boys. Shaw Cross happily moved across to become part of BARLA. As part of the recognition agreement BARLA took over responsibility for organising amateur and youth internationals. It proved to be a hugely beneficial arrangement and many Shaw Cross players went on to enjoy taking part in BARLA teams.

Yorkshire Junior Amateur Rugby League

By the mid-1970s the need for a junior league, outside the jurisdiction of the schools, was clear if all boys were to get a chance of learning the game and taking part in competitive matches. An advertisement was placed in the local press inviting youngsters to come along each Saturday morning to free coaching sessions. Some 140 lads turned up for the first session which was organised at Savile Town by Maurice Bamford, who was then just starting his coaching career at Dewsbury, supported by several of his players and coaches from local amateur clubs such as Shaw Cross. At the end of six Saturday sessions it was decided at a meeting held at Shaw Cross to form a league at under–15 level. All the boys who had taken part were allocated to one of four founder teams – Dewsbury Boys, Dewsbury Moor, Shaw Cross and Thornhill. The competition was then known as the Kirklees Junior Amateur Rugby League, reflecting its immediate boundaries.

Over time the area served expanded, drawing in teams from Castleford, Leeds, Wakefield and York. The age groups covered also expanded to provide fixtures from under–8s to under–15s. To reflect its growth, the competition was renamed the Yorkshire Junior Amateur Rugby League and became the biggest in BARLA. Today, that League organises down to Under–7s level and up to Under–16s. In 2012 the whole of the Yorkshire Junior League switched to summer. It was a switch that prompted a new growth in numbers and by 2016 the League was able to proudly claim that with 100 clubs in membership it was the largest in Europe.

Despite its widening coverage the League is still based at the Shaw Cross Club where it holds regular meetings. Many of the member clubs, like Shaw Cross not only field teams at every age level but also provide the chance for those even younger, the Tots, to play the game on a regular basis

In 1976–77 the club's under–18 team enjoyed a strong run in the Yorkshire Cup. It took a replay in the semi-final to get the better of Huddersfield Supporters and book a place in the final. There the boys came up against another youth team that was closely allied to their town's professional club, Featherstone Supporters. The Featherstone boys, fellow members of the Pennine under–18 league, proved too strong, winning 20–0.

Shaw Cross Tots 2017.

Shaw Cross Under–7s 2017.

Shaw Cross Under–8s 2017. Squad: Sam Anderson, Jacob Hosley, Jacob Bucknell, Odysseus Burnley, Archie Dale, Jimmy Faulkes, Benjamin Finn, Seth Gibson-Fuller, Jack Greenwood, Harvey Hinchliffe, Daniel Jagger, James McCann, Kaiden Mullins, Finley Parker, Cole Stanley, Ben Whitworth, Nathan Ewen, George Kelly, Luke Cartwright, Kayse Rylah, Madeleine Brook, Jack Clarke, Aiden Norman, Rhys Roberts, Archie Thomas, Luke Willert.

Shaw Cross Under–9s 2017. Squad: Alfie Ibbitson, Teddy Dawson, Isaac Redgewick, Toby Turver, Seb Jeffers, Bailey Woods, Phoebe Wilson, Ben Tranter, Harvey Cavanagh, Max Tune, Alfie Law, Charlie Tilford, Casey Hirst, Edan Gleadhill, Dillan Charlton, Jacob Stevenson, Lennon Smith, Jack Stephenson, Frankie Beverley, Eviee Raby, Charlee Raby, Ellis Peake, Francis Appleyard, Ethan Brereton; Coaches: Jo Wilson, Mark Smith, Martin Law, Matty Jeffers.

4. Open age rugby

Up until the mid-1970s, all boys had severed their playing connection with the club on reaching 19 years of age. However, not all the boys were happy to up sticks and join another local club. Quite a number of boys who had played together through Shaw Cross's junior and intermediate teams requested that the club set up an open age section.

One of those boys was Chris Smith and he remembers how it all came about in 1972: "Dave Bradshaw (Brad), our coach at the time, had ideas he could attract a few former players to make up a side and he got hold of a few lads to boost numbers. I remember Tony Martin, Mick Kaye, Tony Cooke, 'Chink' Helliwell, Roger Lees, Glynn Tolson, John Bracken, Tom Buckley, and the youngsters Trevor Scargill, Dave Beevers, Dean Clark, John Birkby, John Haigh, Steve Booth, Martin Summerscales and Graham Smith being among the first to join up and then being joined by a few recruits from Batley including Brian Stenchion, Steve Conway, Bob Kirk, Kevin McGuire and John Temple. The side was born and in the early days was boosted by the addition of Billy Joyner, Neal Clarke, Ashley Livesey, John McGowan, Dave Finnerty and Sam Masson. With them we had a decent side.

In those early days we played at such luxury venues as Todmorden where the sheep had to be scattered from the pitch before the game and the home and away dressing sheds had a tin bath each. Both were filled with hot water and had a tin bucket but you didn't want to be the last player bathing in the mud soup. We were spoilt at Shaw Cross having modern baths and showers. Todmorden got a thrashing when they visited us, but they were chuffed with the baths and showers.

Sadly, today due to medical hygiene baths are no longer allowed but playing away at Siddal was notable as the baths were so deep you could actually swim a few strokes and the water was always piping hot. At a cold, windswept place like Siddal, a warm bath is a huge bonus after playing in wintery conditions with a wind chill factor that felt 10 degrees lower.

We eventually joined BARLA's recently formed Yorkshire League in 1977–78 where Chris Senior was our player-coach. Chris was succeeded by David Ward who was then still Leeds captain before Gary Brook joined our coaching group and we started to progress on to the higher end of the League. Gary made some great progress and brought in some experience. He was a tough taskmaster and wanted his team to be fit and aggressive which he achieved."

Adding an open age team brought with it some unexpected changes to club life. Very quickly the club found itself dealing with the interests of an older group of members for the first time. The open age team very rapidly made itself at home at The Crown at the bottom of Leeds Road where a former Shaw Cross junior, Bob Walker, was landlord. Effectively it became their headquarters.

Different amenities were quickly needed if the club was to stay together. Plans were drawn up and a £10,000 brewery loan was accepted to enable work to get underway. Driven on by Trevor Scargill, a small extension was added to the club house where a licensed bar was opened in 1982. There a social club developed that would provide a much appreciated meeting place and much needed revenue for the club in the coming years.

After consolidating its place in the Yorkshire League, the open age team gained promotion to its Senior Division in 1987. By then an 'A' team had been formed and it rapidly gained honours, winning the second division of the Yorkshire League and the Heavy Woollen Cup in its first season.

Two years after establishing the elite National Amateur Rugby League, BARLA asked for entries for places in the new second division that was to be launched in 1989–90. The selection criteria for membership deliberately demanded high minimum standards and this worked in favour of those clubs like Shaw Cross which not only ran reserve and under–18 teams but also had good facilities. Shaw Cross was elected and became the League's first member and for a short while the only member from the Heavy Woollen district. That was to prove short-lived because before the new league kicked off one of the original members dropped out and Dewsbury Celtic was brought in as the second.

With new opponents to face in Cumbria and Greater Manchester it was important that the team made a good impression. Mick Turner's company stepped in provide to shirts, ties and jumpers for all the squad. They were delivered in three bin liners to the clubhouse on the Thursday before the League got underway on the Saturday. When Saturday came no one could find the bin liners. Unfortunately, the cleaners had not realised what they contained and thrown all three in the skip. Another set had to be prepared for the following week.

Winners and losers

Douglas Hird remembers one particularly moment in the club' history: "Shaw Cross Sharks over the years have been renowned for their successes on the rugby field, winning numerous trophies, particularly at junior and youth level. But few will remember in one year an under– 15s team at Shaw Cross went through a whole season without winning a match. Keith Foster was the coach of that side.

I read in the press of a similar team in Blackpool that had also failed to win a game all season and decided they should play one another and at least one of them would finish with a victory. Keith took his side to Blackpool and you know what, the Shaw Cross boys were defeated in that match.

Keith was no quitter, he had faith in his team, but he knew the players would be disappointed at the annual club presentation night when other teams were receiving their awards. Unknown to anyone, Keith, an engineer, set about making a little trophy for each player which he engraved with just two words 'Gallant Losers' and these were duly presented at the presentation night in Dewsbury Town Hall.

Ironically, these 'special trophies' which of course were unique, became the most revered at the club and the following season this Shaw Cross team started to win their games. It was a happy ending for those boys who will always remember the little bit of history they made, however painful it might have been."

Juniors

By the start of the 1990s Shaw Cross was enjoying a mini boom, turning out teams every week at under–8, under–9, under–11, under–13 and under–15 levels. And when the season ended the club put on a summer school so that those youngsters could learn even more about the game. Central to that good work was a team of qualified coaches who had the necessary training to instil in the youngsters the skills of the game. They were also keen to instil in the youngsters the disciplines of the game and a strict 'no train, no play' policy was enforced.

However, there was a strong feeling that the club was stagnating. Its largest group of members were in the junior sections who had only one seat on the committee. If the club was to move forward there was a need for change and that the juniors should be given a stronger voice in what was effectively an open age club. Nigel Walsh, a former junior who had returned to the club from Hanging Heaton, worked with Mick Turner to draw up a new committee structure which would give all parts of the club an equal voice in how it should be run and where it should be heading. It gave three seats to the juniors, three seats to the open age and three seats for the overall club officers, the secretary, treasurer and chairman. It proved to be the right answer and helped to reinvigorate the club.

The junior section was reorganised and a group of enthusiastic members – Sue Bell, Dean Ellis, Kevin Millington, Angie Myers and Alan Smith – formed the basis of a new junior committee and took responsibility for managing and raising its own money. A junior disco started in the old clubhouse. Run by Nigel Walsh, Mick and Mandy Turner, Andy and Sue Bell, Kevin and Pauline Millington and Dean and Sue Ellis it proved very popular and not only gave the old clubhouse a new lease of life but also provided a welcome revenue stream. Another popular innovation was an annual bonfire night firework display.

Over the years many people have become involved with the junior section when their children have joined the club. Some have continued their voluntary work long after their children have moved on. Angela Myers and Dean Ellis are just two of those people who are still very much involved. Angela is a past chairman of the junior section and is now treasurer of the club. And just for good measure she cooks the food for the after match refreshments at the NCL home matches. As mentioned above, Dean's service began more than twenty years ago when he helped with the junior discos. Today, he serves on the executive committee and is involved in the running of the Shaw Cross Social Club.

The first Open Age side: Back: Glynn Tolson, Trevor Scargill, Chris Smith, Bob Kirk, Gurdy Ryatt, Ian Helliwell, Brian Stenchion, John Temple, John Birkby, Dean Clarke, David Bradshaw (Coach); front: Stuart Booth, Tony Martin, Mick Kaye, Tom Buckley, Dave Ellis, John Haig, Chris Halloran, Steve Conway, John Bracken.

Yorkshire Youth Top four play–offs winners 1985–86: Back: Bernard Watson (Coach), Daz Basto, Kevin Enwright, Andy Watson, Phil Sykes, Richard Medley, Ian Bottomley, Steve Garnett, Simon Thompson, Aidy Ripley (Assistant Coach); front: Mark Grundell, Lee Roberts, Jonny Ripley, Mark Hardy, Terry McGuire, Karl Humphries, John Lumb.

Shaw Cross open age team 1990: Back: Wayne Bastow, Steve Barrick, Steve Naylor, Graham Marsden, Andrew Wood, Richard Gregory, Gurdy Ryatt, Phil Sykes; front: Mark Grundell, Simon Robertshaw, Darryl Bastow, Adrian Ripley, Andrew Nelmes, Jonathan Ripley, Roger Toole.

Shaw Cross Open Age 'A' Team in 1990.

Since those early days the junior section has continued to grow and develop its activities. A gala for seven to 11 year olds playing nine-a-side has been held for over a decade and in August 2015 attracted over 450 people. By that time the juniors were fielding 13 boys teams between tots and under–16s and two girls teams. It is a remarkable achievement to provide so many matches and training sessions each week in a fun environment.

Of course, it only happens because Alan Smith who is now the secretary of the junior section can call upon a huge volunteer effort. Under the current guidelines each of those teams requires its own manager, coach, first aider and touchline manager all of whom have had to be Disclose and Barring Service (DBS) checked to ensure that they can work with young people. The club prides itself on the role its volunteers play. It is rightly proud that throughout the season a group of parents provide meals for their own children's age group after all junior and youth matches.

Near neighbours Dewsbury Rams have been an active supporter of Shaw Cross's activities over the years. James Stephenson who was the under–9s coach at the time, devised a scheme to develop local talent and got the Rams on board. Named the Mentoring and Development Scheme, it saw the Rams players become personally involved in providing positional coaching for the Shaw Cross juniors. The scheme was launched in April 2009 but foundered not long after James Stephenson began a career first with Dewsbury Rams and shortly afterwards Wakefield Trinity Wildcats.

Support for the club's efforts is also provided by two local Super League clubs. Shaw Cross is linked with the Huddersfield Giants Community Trust and since 2013 has been an ambassador club for the Leeds Rhinos Foundation. In addition the club has also been involved with rugby camps beginning with Paul Sculthorpe and more recently both Paul March and Jamie Peacock.

With so many youngsters involved, so many volunteers giving their time and support from the professional game everything appears extremely positive but there are some dark clouds on the horizon as Chris Smith, the club chairman explains: "The early Academy set up was not a major issue with us as it involved under–18 to 19 players so it was not too harmful to junior rugby. The current system though is different in that they scout talent at under–12 and under–13 to play under–U15 and under–16 rugby. This takes out far too many junior players from clubs who are often left without a team at these age groups and subsequently don't have under–16s, – 17s or –18s going forward. The high numbers taken result in high numbers released at 18 who often do not return to play open age. In our experience they take lads who are physically strong at 13 to 14 years old but not always the most talented. When the rest catch up physically many are found to lack the skills needed to progress, hence the high turnover.

Initially the professional clubs used to simply coach the under–15 and under–16 players and monitor them with their junior clubs, then they introduced leagues and began playing games which prevented them from playing junior club rugby during the season. This is the current set up and harms the junior game and player retention. Also many talented players are overlooked too young because they are less physically mature and scouts these days tend not to watch under–16 and under17 rugby as they perceive the talent has already been cherry picked from the side. I personally would prefer to see reserve rugby return when clubs could take a player at age 16 to 18 on trial for a four or six match period then sign them or allow them to return to their club."

It is a major issue for the amateur game and one that needs attention both for the impact mass recruitment has in the first place and also because of the losses that the game suffers when young players, not signed after their Academy years are over, do not return to their roots.

Professional academies are not the only concern. Over the past year there has been a debate arising from the growing concern about the drop off in participation numbers amongst the late teens. It has always been a problem area as outside influences vie for a young player's time. Rugby league has to fight for its share of that time against many newer home based alternatives such as games consoles and IPads. Some however feel that by the time a lad reaches 18 and has progressed right through the age groups since mini-rugby that he may have almost played too much and is ready for a break. It is another issue for the community game to grapple with.

National Conference League

In the aftermath of a special meeting of the RFL in March 1993, which reorganised the competition and cut Blackpool Gladiators, Chorley Borough and Nottingham Outlaws from its ranks, the RFL in partnership with BARLA announced plans for a new three division National Amateur Rugby League. This would henceforth be known as the National Conference League. The introduction of the three former professional clubs caused a re-organisation of the membership and saw three members, including Shaw Cross Sharks, pushed downwards into the new League's second division alongside seven newcomers.

After surviving re-election at the end of that first season, the Sharks went on to gain promotion to the first division in 1997. Before then there had been major developments at the club.

The Paul Hinchliffe Memorial Playing Fields

Paul Hinchliffe joined Shaw Cross as a youngster and was playing with the under–19s when he was taken ill. He was diagnosed with leukaemia and sadly died one week before his 21st birthday in 1993. Paul's death was a shock to all at the club and following discussions with the local council it was agreed to rename the Grange Road playing fields as the Paul Hinchliffe Memorial Playing Fields. A large boulder complete with plaque was erected near the entrance to the playing fields.

A new clubhouse

As the new season got underway in August 1996 the members had much to be proud of. Club members had banded together over the summer to improve the playing facilities at the club's ground, installing fencing and two new dugouts. The Mayor of Kirklees was on hand to open the ground improvements for the visit of Skirlaugh at the end of the month and the club seemed set fair for further progress.

Then two months later the club suffered a huge blow when fire ripped through the clubhouse. Thousands of pounds worth of damage was caused and nearly 50 years-worth of irreplaceable trophies, banners, kits and records were destroyed. The fire had been caused by a break-in during the night and the cause was thought to be a discarded cigarette. Some matches had to be postponed and methods of raising much needed cash were soon being investigated.

Unfortunately, the club was not in the best possible position financially. When the possibility of raising a mortgage was discussed it rapidly became clear that with debts to the brewery of around £7,000 and the clubhouse valued at only £9,000 it was not a viable option. Other ways would have to be found.

Within a few months an application for a National Lottery grant had been prepared and in August 1997 came the good news that it had been successful. The club was able to celebrate its 50th birthday with a grant of £281,000, around 90 per cent of the estimated cost, towards developing its own new premises. There was one prerequisite before the grant was made. A boys' club on its own was too narrow. To receive the money the club had to widen its appeal to young people of both sexes and so the Shaw Cross Club for Young People came into being.

The site for the new clubhouse was the club's old training area. Brian Clarke, recently retired from the police, and Mick Turner took on the mountain of administrative work needed and John Lyttle's company Jay-Tee Construction took on the building work. Douglas Hird was on hand to lay the foundation stone on 20 March 1998. Eight months later, Mike Stephenson returned to officially open the new two-storey club house.

Sports Club of the Year

All this good work had not gone unnoticed. In November 1998, Shaw Cross was chosen by BARLA as its nominee for the 'Sports Club of the Year' award presented by the Foundation for Sports and the Arts and the Central Council of Physical Recreation. A four-man delegation – Douglas Hird, Alan Lancaster, Nigel Walsh and Mick Turner – set off for the award night more in hope than anticipation.

The judges at the presentation dinner at Huntingdon in Cambridgeshire endorsed BARLA's belief that "Shaw Cross is a shining example of the type of community based club upon which amateur rugby league thrives" and named it their club of the year which brought with it a first prize of £10,000. In his acceptance speech Douglas stressed that the club was not just to turn its junior players into rugby league players but to make them players at both the game and life beyond.

There was more good fortune to come that night. A raffle was held and when it came to the draw first Douglas won a prize, then Alan won a bottle of whisky and finally Mick won the big prize on the night, two return flights to New York. Only Nigel had missed out or so he thought. Mick left it so late to make arrangements that his tickets were about to expire and his wife could not accompany him. Another travelling companion had to be found at short notice and this time Nigel struck lucky. The pair enjoyed their trip to the Big Apple, although neither of their partners was amused.

Three years later an £80,000 extension was opened which provided a new players' gymnasium and above it a members' bar, that was named the Douglas M Hird Suite. This extension was made possible thanks to a £70,000 grant. This came from the Biffa Awards via the Landfill Communities Fund.

Sportsman's Dinner in 2011: Peter Emmett, Paul Sculthorpe, Mike Stephenson, Lee Gilmour and Olivier Elima.

5. International links

Shaw Cross has always tried to foster rugby league's international links and in support of that aim has played matches in many parts off the world.

Douglas is the key person to explain how the club's French connection came about: "The pioneering spirit of Shaw Cross was responsible for establishing the link across the English Channel with France in 1969 which led to the Yorkshire Association of Boys' Clubs French rugby league Exchange being set up. The first positive move came from Shaw Cross. Chairman Alan Lancaster met Monsieur Gilbert Dautant, who organised his country's amateur team, in Manchester and discussed the possibility of organising a regular rugby league exchange with the French.

The French were delighted with the suggestion and decided it should be based at Villeneuve-sur-Lot, the birthplace of French rugby league. It was also agreed that the Yorkshire Association of Boys' Clubs Exchange should be based at Shaw Cross and the following year the exchange was born. Gilbert Dautant became the co-ordinator on the French side of the Exchange.

Over Easter 1970, led by Alan Lancaster, Douglas Hird and Trevor Foster, the former Bradford Northern international forward then serving as assistant leader at the Bradford Police Boys' Club, the first Yorkshire boys' squad made the historic and pioneering journey to Lot-et-Garonne region of south west France. It was fitting that that small town should be the cradle of the Yorkshire Boys' Exchange and the link was firmly established, with the Yorkshire boys and the French boys making alternative year trips to one another's country."

In those days, long before the high speed TGV train service, this was an arduous journey. The club's party of one team plus reserves headed south to Dover and then took the ferry across to Calais. Then they set off by train for Paris where after a change of stations they journeyed on to south west France. There was still over 500 kilometres to go to reach their destination; Villeneuve, an important commercial centre, stands on the River Lot midway between Bordeaux and Toulouse.

Alighting at Penn station they were met with great pomp and ceremony before being billeted with French families for the duration of their stay.

Three matches had been arranged, one at Villeneuve and two others at nearby Tonneins and Casseneuil. The first two matches ended in defeat, 16–11 and 27–20 respectively, before the third was won 11–3. Each match was followed by a civic reception. In addition to the matches and a number of educational and cultural visits, the hospitality provided by their French hosts was remembered long after the tour was over.

The following year a party of French boys were invited over to Yorkshire. The invitation was accepted eagerly. As Douglas recounted "Instead of one squad of 20 boys returning, they asked to bring two squads of Under–16 and Under–18 players, making 40 in total which should be the basis for the exchange in future.

First French Tour Squad 1970: Dean Bostock, Ian Brook, David Dyson, Robert Farrar, David Field, Stephen Godfrey, Roger Guy (Captain) Andrew Hodson, Stephen Johnson, Brian Kane, Brian Lockwood, Keith Mumby, Nigel Owens, Duncan Oxley, Colin Robinson. Andrew Smith, Ian Waring.

France Tour 1978: Leaders: Alan Lancaster, Douglas Hird, Darrel Ellison, Ged Birkin; Squad: Michael Aitcheson, Frank Barratt, Richard Butterworth, Mark Burgess, Paul Brown, Neal Clarke, Stephen Cooper, Martin Coulthard, John Clapham, Stephen Douglas, Sean Fallon, Gary Fisher, Peter Fothergill, Nigel Gibson, Andrew Hall, Wayne Heron, Phillip Hirst, Bernard Kilroy, Sean Lockhead, Chris Messenger, Steve Mellor, John McGowan, Graham Marsden, Neil Maddison, Ian Mckintosh, Andrew Mckintosh, Ian Mills, Leo Moorhouse, Ian Nowlands, Adrian Ripley, Darryl Senior, Gary Shaw, David Slater, Graham Smith, Andrew Stott, Gary Tasker, Mark Todd, Nigel Walsh, Shaun Webster, James Wood.

France Tour 1990: Leaders: Alan Lancaster, Douglas Hird, Chris Smith, Mick Gibson; Squad: John Agar, Michael Armitage, Richard Bainton, Richard Barker, Wayne Bastow, Craig Beaumont, John Biggs, Terry Bishop, Alan Brown, Darren Collins, Robert Danby, Ryan Davies, Gary Duke, Adam Eccles, Daniel Farey, Glen Freeman, Wayne Freeman, Darren Grannon, Richard Gregory, Crispian Havercroft, Richard Hewitt, Simon Kirk, Anthony Lemon, David Mckay, Daniel Marquex-Laynez, Mark Milnes, Richard O'Brien, Craig O'Donnell, Anthony Oldridge, Colin Page, Gary Pollard, Robert Simpson, Ian Strangeway, Christopher Verity, Neil Wardrobe, Andrew Woolford, Ian Wright.

French and Shaw Cross group leaders 1992: Chris Smith, Mick Gibson, Alain Dureac, Douglas Hird, Alan Lancaster, Claude Frayssinous, Jack Fort.

We agreed, but two days before their arrival in Dewsbury we received an urgent telephone call, saying a further 20 boys were on their way, making a party of 60.

These additional 20 French lads should have gone to Warrington, but the Lancashire officials had had to cancel their tour at the 11th hour, virtually leaving the French boys stranded after they had made their travelling arrangements.

The 40-strong original party all stayed with local families in Dewsbury, Ossett, Batley and Bradford. To house the additional party, the Council agreed to turn Shaw Cross Junior School into a makeshift boarding house while the adjacent Boys' Club with its own catering facilities provided their canteen. On their first visit the French played matches against Shaw Cross, Dewsbury and Batley schoolboys and Ossett Trinity." The exchange was up and running.

In the early days the party represented the Yorkshire Association of Boys' Clubs and included some on occasion representatives from the Bradford Police, Bradford Sedbergh, Hunslet and Hull clubs. Eventually the tour would not only be organised by Shaw Cross but would be mostly composed of Shaw Cross boys. However, over the years the tour party has been augmented by members of the Hull Boys Club, the Hunslet Boys Club and Hunslet Parkside. When the French boys have played over here other opponents have been added to their itinerary and for many years matches against West Hull were included.

It is never straightforward taking a party of young lads to France. There was a potential major problem on one tour as Douglas recalls: "I will never forget an incident which occurred on one of the early tours on our French exchange which could have threatened the future of tours to France. The occasion was when the young players had to stay one night in a local school before being allocated to French families in Villeneuve.

Early the next morning I found the row of washbasins were full of water and swimming with numerous large goldfish. I quickly realised where they had come from – an ornamental pool in the main street but how had they got there! What should I do? These goldfish were the pride of the Mayor and they would soon be missed. Quick action was needed if a calamity was to be avoided. I told the players: 'I don't want to know who were responsible but no one will get breakfast this morning until those goldfish are back in the pond.' I immediately went across to the hotel and told the cook to serve no boys until I returned.

Needless to say the goldfish were soon swimming in the pond again. How they managed to get them back I do not know or who were the culprits. Fortunately no hurt was caused to the French and the boys all got their breakfast."

As the exchange approached its 30th anniversary there was a major change in the travel arrangements. Long distance coaches and even trains became transports of the past. Thanks to the opening up of European airspace it was possible in 1998 for the party to fly to France for the first time. Now, the boys fly from Liverpool to Bergerac in the Dordogne before completing the journey with a short drive south.

The exchanges have always proved popular and no more so than in late 2015 when an extra tour took place. Having enjoyed their previous visit, a group of Under–

17s decided they would like to return to France. Contact was made with the French organisers and a nines contest was arranged. A party of nine headed across the Channel from Shaw Cross to play in a tournament against Villeneuve and Tonneins.

Allez Shaw Cross 2016

The 47th exchange saw the Shaw Cross boys back in France in 2016. Ahead of the tour serious fund-raising got underway. One of the main fundraising events was titled 'Pedal to Pujols'. Thanks to the generosity of the Village Hotel in nearby Tingley, a group of boys were able to pedal the equivalent distance to Pujols in the Hotel's fitness room. The boys were well sponsored and completed the distance in two weeks. Other fund-raising events included race nights and a bag pack at a nearby Morrisons supermarket, all topped up with sponsorship cash from local companies.

Although foreign travel is more commonplace, the trip across Channel is still a great adventure providing not just the opportunity to play a couple of matches abroad but also a wealth of new experiences. However, holidays are only a partial preparation for the challenges presented by a week coping with a foreign language, homesickness and on the occasion the food.

In 2016 the party of 25 boys and six coaches and leaders set off on Good Friday for a week as usual in the Lot valley. On landing at Bergerac the party was divided up, the boys going on to room with families in either Villeneuve-sur-Lot or Tonneins. The coaches and leaders had their own accommodation on a camp site at Villeneuve.

In days gone by the tour often took in matches against other small towns in the area such as Pujols or St Lavarde or Trentels but none are able to put youth teams on the field these days. French rugby league is not only weaker in numbers. Those clubs that remain active are struggling for numbers in the age groups involved. There are fewer players and many have been brought through the local rugby union ranks. The 2016 tour saw the new French organisers, Sebastien Gauffre and Julien Mourer, arrange for the Shaw Cross Under–14 and Under–15 teams to play the Villeneuve Under–15s and Under–16s, before playing the same age groups at Tonneins.

Bienvenue a Shaw Cross 2017

During Easter 2017, the French boys arrived back in West Yorkshire. The task of organising their visit fell to a small committee. Following the retirement of the founders, Douglas Hird and Alan Lancaster, the organisation of the French Exchange has been taken over by Alan Smith and Tracy Grimwood. Alan Smith, who has been chairman for twenty-two years, Tracy Grimwood, who acts as treasurer, and her daughter Katie make up the small committee. There is less flexibility about the tour dates these days because of the different dates set by the surrounding local education authorities for the Easter holidays. They started work in early January.

37

Tracy is responsible for the critical task of arranging accommodation because without member meeting the need there can be no tour. As the club has a duty of care for the visiting boys, only club members can volunteer and only families are considered to provide accommodation. It is a demanding job and Tracy started looking for volunteers right away. Those who had volunteered before were the first target but inevitably the net had to be widened to meet the demand. With just two weeks to go there were still nine boys to house but as before Tracy found places for them all in time. This year the boys were assigned to 25 homes.

For the families involved it's a busy week. They not only provide accommodation and socialise with the boys on an evening but can if they wish volunteer to be part of the tour's daily activities. It's not just the families who are kept busy. The French tour leaders stay at a local hotel but each evening they are 'fed and watered' by one of the leaders of the previous year's Shaw Cross party.

Once the French organisers have confirmed the numbers and age range of the boys in their party, normally a month before their arrival, a detailed tour itinerary is prepared. This year's itinerary was as action packed as always.

The party of 38 boys and six tour leaders arrived at East Midlands Airport on Easter Sunday morning. After a short journey by coach and lunch the boys were ready for two matches against Shaw Cross under–15s and later the under–16s. Besides giving the boys their first taste of British rugby league those matches also give the organisers the chance to assess their standard and to rearrange the age groups of their future opponents to prevent possible mismatches.

Having played their first matches the boys were able to travel over to Headingley the following evening to watch Leeds Rhinos take on the Widnes Vikings. Tuesday was another rest day and the boys spent the day swimming and ice skating at Doncaster Dome. Matches against Batley Boys under–13s an under–16s were arranged at Shaw Cross on the Wednesday. Thanks to the support of Northern Rail the boys spent Thursday at Blackpool's Pleasure Beach before winding up the tour with matches against Shaw Cross under–14s and under–15s the following day. Saturday saw the party fly home from Liverpool.

As usual the tour went well and the feedback to Tracy from all involved showed just how much the week had been enjoyed.

It has been a remarkable series of exchanges which has seen nearly 2,000 boys involved. That involvement has helped many young players on their way to professional Rugby League. And not just in this country. There have been many future top players amongst the French tour parties. Over the years, a number of future internationals, such as Gilles Dumas, Laurent Frayssinous, Kain Bentley, Mickael Simon, William Barthau, Laurent Carrasco and Oliver Elima, could be found in the tour parties.

It has been traditional to name a 'Player of the Tour' after each visit to France. In 2002 this was marked with a prestigious trophy when the former Great Britain captain Ellery Hanley donated one of the two 'Man of Steel' silver trophies he won during his illustrious professional career to the club. Ellery visited the club in 2002 to make the first presentation. The winners so far have been:

2002: Tom Colleran
2004: Luke Haigh
2006: Tom Wall
2008: Jake Wilson
2010: Thomas Ripley
2012: Nick Davies
2014: Jack Flynn
2016: Harry Bowes.

Australia and New Zealand

Looking for an appropriate way to celebrate Shaw Cross's 30th birthday, the club's leadership came up with the idea of organising a tour of Australasia in 1977 to coincide with the Queen's Silver Jubilee. It was a bold move and one that no other amateur club had attempted in the game's 82 year history. Sponsorship was sought to meet the costs, which were estimated at £750 for each member of the playing party. Did the Sports Council make a contribution?

In fact, sensing it was almost too bold financially, Shaw Cross officials approached BARLA for support. A meeting was arranged with Maurice Oldroyd, the national administrator, where it was agreed that BARLA would take over the responsibility for the under–18 tour but, in recognition of the work put in to planning the trip already carried out by Shaw Cross, the tour would be led by two club officials, Douglas Hird and Alan Lancaster, and included two players, Graham Smith and James Wood, in the 20 strong party.

Sufficient funds were raised in time for the pioneering party to gather at a Wilmslow hotel for dinner with senior BARLA officials. On the following afternoon, 3 June, the party departed from Manchester Airport bound for Auckland. After stops at Los Angeles, Honolulu and Suva the party arrived at their destination on the morning of 5 June.

There was little time for acclimatisation as the players were transported over to Carlaw Park to watch the World Cup clash between Great Britain and France. After that the party was thrown into the fray. Two matches were played in New Zealand – one against Northern Zone in Auckland and one against a New Zealand XIII in Christchurch, which was played as a curtain-raiser to the New Zealand versus Great Britain World Cup match.

Then, it was time to fly on to Australia to meet a Toowoomba District team. Next up was an Illawarra District team before finally meeting an Australian XIII at the Sydney Cricket Ground as a curtain-raiser for the World Cup final between Australia and Great Britain. Two days later it was time for the party to say farewell and begin the long journey home via Singapore, Kula Lumpur and Bahrein.

Shaw Cross French tour squad in the late 1990s.

Shaw Cross French Tour squad in the early 2000s.

Shaw Cross and French boys 2002.

Shaw Cross and Villeneuve in 2004.

Laurent Carrasco presents one of his international shirts to Sam Ottewell on the
Shaw Cross tour to France in 2012.

Jack Fort, Tracy Grimwood, Douglas Hird, Alan Smith and Alain Daureac. Jack and Alain had been given Life Membership of the Shaw Cross club.

International rugby league manager and super star athlete:
Mick Turner and Usain Bolt on a BARLA tour of Jamaica.

While the final record may have shown four defeats and a single draw against the New Zealand XIII, the tour had been a testing but valuable experience. That pioneering tour, conceived by Shaw Cross, had been a rousing success and created a great deal of interest 'Down Under'. Not only did it spur both Australia and New Zealand to begin seriously considering youth tours to England but also led BARLA to make such tours a regular future highlight of the domestic game.

Wanderlust

Prior to becoming coach of Shaw Cross Sharks, Mick Turner was dispatched to South Africa by BARLA as a British Ambassador for Sport ahead of its first tour there in 1993. His job was to help in preparing teams in Cape Town and Johannesburg to take on the touring North Sydney Bears. On that initial visit Mick met the local development officer, Martin Birmingham who had begun his involvement with rugby league at Dewsbury Celtic. Martin offered invites for any clubs willing to make the trip to Cape Town. Mick, a former junior who had returned to the club from Dewsbury Norths, brought the opportunity back to Shaw Cross where it was accepted enthusiastically.

Having decided they would go, there was just the issue of raising the cash to address. Although an odd event or two was held to raise funds, nearly the whole of the tour cost was borne by the players and officials themselves.

Ahead of the tour playing kit, equipment and souvenirs were collected and transported out to South Africa for distribution. From the professional side, St Helens and Warrington were among the most generous.

The pioneering club tour took place in May 1999. Cape Town Cobras would provide the Sharks' main opposition on this tour as they would in future. The Sharks had to make a rapid readjustment to the local conditions and they did it well enough to win one match and draw the other while on tour. The Sharks' opponents, nearly all local rugby union men, were obviously inexperienced in the ways of league but very enthusiastic. The facilities on the whole were modest, mostly open hard grounds. However, the accommodation was good and the food was fine.

As well as playing rugby league, the Sharks visited schools in the African townships and provided coaching. These were coaching sessions with a difference. Held on basic open fields, the Shaw Cross coaches had to work hard to organise lots of barefoot kids all eager to get involved. From the noise they made it was obvious just how much they were enjoying the chance to try rugby league.

It was while providing coaching at a school in the township of Elsie's River that a car pulled up two streets away and opened fire, killing one man and injuring two others. A police helicopter was soon overhead and the Shaw Cross party was provided with a police escort out of the area. As Chris Smith told reporters at the time "It turned out to be one of the most exciting coaching sessions we have ever had". It was all not rugby league. Time was made for trips to the beach and a couple of trips were made to see some of the spectacular scenery of the Cape Province.

Further tours followed in 2001 and 2003. Teams met were Cape Town Cobras and Western Province. On one occasion the Sharks played a match at rugby union club in Cape Town where the facilities were quite good both on and off the field.

Two of the opposition's players in the final game of the 2003 tour – Bradley Green and Marius Schwarts – later travelled to England to trial for the Dewsbury Rams. Both appeared for Dewsbury Colts but sadly neither could make the first-team. Instead both turned out for the Sharks, Bradley for quite a while, before returning to the Cape.

At the start of May 2005 the club toured Serbia and Montenegro where the interest in the game had been rekindled after a long break. The tour opened on Easter Monday with a double header in Belgrade, the Sharks entering two teams into a seven-a-side tournament which was then followed by a full match between the Sharks and a Belgrade Select XIII which the Sharks won easily 48–10. Three days later the Sharks met the Vojvodina Rams at Novi Sad where they won 80–6.

An enjoyable visit to Serbia was made even more memorable by a chance encounter with Grace Jones in a Heathrow departure lounge. Although the international film star and singer refused requests for photographs she did agree to sign autographs, shirts and even the blow up Sharks' mascot. She also said she would speak to her publicist on arrival and arrange for the party to attend her open air concert in Belgrade. She was as good as her word and the Sharks had a great time. Also while on tour Mick Turner and Ryan Halloran appeared on state television and were later guests of the British Consul where diplomats thanked them for being great ambassadors for their country, club and the game of Rugby League.

To celebrate the club's Diamond Jubilee two years later, the Sharks decided to visit another European country where the game was just getting going. This time a party paid a flying visit to the Czech Republic. The party arrived in Prague on Friday and played a match that same evening, beating a Czech Republic under–23 XIII 64–18. There was so little money available for the organisers that no post-match food was available and the Shaw Cross party had to have a whip round before eating. Having got the rugby out of the way the party was then able to enjoy the delights of Prague before flying home on Sunday.

6. Summer rugby

The professional game made an abrupt switch to so-called summer rugby in the autumn of 1995. From the following year, the game's highest professional clubs were playing a season that ran from February to October.

At first the senior amateur game stayed aloof, but at Shaw Cross the junior teams made the switch. Most enjoyed the experience, so it was only a matter of time before those juniors were of an age when senior summer rugby would have to be considered.

Early in 2010, at a time when Shaw Cross was briefly the only NCL outfit in the area for a couple of years after Thornhill Trojans dropped out, the RFL announced that a widespread consultation would take place to determine what amateur clubs and leagues thought of the playing season. Although most were still playing in the winter the possibility of a move to a summer season was seen part of the motive for the consultation.

The NCL consulted its members about a move to summer over 2010–11. With bad weather causing havoc, fixtures were virtually wiped out between November and February, Shaw Cross was one of the clubs who voted by quite a big majority to switch to summer.

To test the water the club took the opportunity to place a team in the expanded Yorkshire Premier Division of the Rugby League Conference for summer 2011. It proved a popular move with the existing players and even attracted some new ones.

All that was left to do to make the switch was for the NCL to organise an interim regional winter season in late 2011 in readiness for the first summer season which would run from March to November 2012.

It was a major change for amateur clubs to make and many had to negotiate with their landlords their possible change of usage. In Shaw Cross's case the negotiations with Kirklees Council went smoothly over the Grange Road playing field and with a group of players on board summer rugby could begin.

Looking back, Douglas remembers that many foresaw problems with summer rugby: "Leisure activities would inevitably affect player availability and it was felt that the club would need greater strength in depth to successfully run a senior squad supporting a first and a reserve team. We were happily surprised by the way the club adapted to summer rugby. Players continued to make themselves available and we had hardly any postponements due our inability to raise a team."

2013 – A cause for celebration

There was a double cause for celebration towards the end of 2013. Thanks to 44–18 win against Leigh East, the Sharks gained promotion from Division Two as runner up, making up for narrowly missing out the previous year.

Shaw Cross Open Age – Darryl Woollen winners in 2003.

A confident looking NCL Shaw Cross Open Age squad.

Shaw Cross Sharks Open Age team – 2004–05 NCL Division 1 Champions.

An Open Age squad showing the alternative kits.

A Shaw Cross Ladies team before a charity match in 2002.

Shaw Cross Under–15s 2004–05.

Then, at the RFL Community Awards ceremony at Old Trafford the club was one of the winners announced as part of the Rugby League Cares' Engage with your Club programme. It was an honour, bestowed by a programme which celebrated work undertaken on improving a club's facilities that also brought with it a much appreciated cash award.

Goodbye to winter

For a short while Shaw Cross ran both winter and summer teams. The winter team played in BARLA's Pennine League until 2014–15. That proved to be the last winter season as player interest had completely switched to summer.

Shaw Cross withdrew from the Pennine League and switched its reserves to the Yorkshire Men's League. With that the club was wholly committed to summer but it is always possible that a team will maybe return to winter one day.

That does not mean that all the club's members have dropped their interest in the winter game. Some open age players switch each year at the end of the summer season to continue playing over the winter with other clubs before returning in the spring to Shaw Cross.

Two years on Shaw Cross remain the highest placed Dewsbury team, playing in NCL Division One. Also in membership are Thornhill Trojans in Division Two and Dewsbury Celtic and Dewsbury Moor Maroons who reside this season in Division Three. The Sharks' reserve team this year finds itself in the NCL Alliance, a new competition for NCL reserve team run by the Yorkshire Men's League.

Left: John Rourke breaks through against Eastmoor.

Middle: Casey Johnson tries a back flip.

Bottom: Sam Ottewell and Ben Spaven stop Oulton Raiders.

On the attack against Thornhill Trojans.

Andrew Masson runs into Oulton Raiders.

Here come the girls

Claiming that there was no other club in the area to cater for their interests, a group of girls sent a deputation to the management committee who agreed to admit them as members for a trial period in 1977. Although they were barred from rugby league those pioneering girls did represent the Boys' club in a five-a-side association football competition at Cleckheaton Sports Centre.

The girls' football team did not last much longer. There was a brief chance for women's rugby when the Thornhill Trojans' women's team relocated across to Shaw Cross but only for a season before disbanding. The lack of an actual girls' team did not stop young girls being interested in the game. That interest was there as Natalie Gilmour remembers: "I started playing rugby at about eight years old at Shaw Cross. My cousin Mick Turner was a coach there and my brother Lee also played there. I had to play in the boys' team as there were no girls teams way back then. I played in the same team as Lee, he was a skinny half-back and I played in the pack.

I played for Shaw Cross up until 11 years old when girls and boys weren't allowed to play in the same team. As there were no girls' teams around, I had to play other sports so I took up hockey and football. I played football for Leeds United, and played for England under–16 at hockey.

When I was 18 years old my cousin Mick mentioned he'd just been on a coaching course with a female rugby coach for a women's team. He gave me her contact details, I went along and trained and that was it, I had the rugby bug back. It was Wakefield Panthers that I played for. They're the only team I've played for, although we've changed our name a few times and are now Featherstone Ladies.

I made my international debut in 1998, with my last international in the World Cup in 2013 when I decided to hang up my international boots. During my international career I've played in numerous World Cups and competed in a number of tours to France, Australia and New Zealand. I actually don't know how many caps I have!

My parents were so supportive, as both Lee and I played rugby, with Lee turning professional. They had to take us everywhere, my mum would take one of us with my dad taking the other to our respective team games. If it wasn't for them I wouldn't have been able to reach the levels I did, the longevity I had and been honoured with both The RFL Roll of Honour and an MBE. I owe a massive thank you to all of them."

Since then female interest has been officially rekindled and the club has been able to develop an under–14 and under–16 girls' teams. Thanks to work undertaken by the Leeds Rhinos Foundation at nearby Woodkirk Academy an under–12 girls team has now been launched. This year will see under–12 and under–14 teams competing in the Yorkshire Girls Amateur Rugby League competition. There are hopes for the future with age group teams feeding an enthusiastic under–16 team that a women's open age team came be set up some time in the future.

Natalie Gilmour, playing for England, leaving a French opponent behind.

Shaw Cross Under–14s Girls Blacks. Squad: Olivia Saczok, Devon Oldroyd, Eleanor Dawson, Immy Payne, Ebony Walshaw, Amelie Carter, Maya Briggs, Kizzie Senior, Kacie Timmins, Millie Dearn, Lydia Fawkes, Alice Inwood, Lauren Mowatt, Lily-Mai Hirst, Ebony Briggs, Courtney Marsh, Cody-Lou Marsh, Paige Wheater, Abigail Pinder; Coach: Andrew Fawkes.

Shaw Cross Under–14s Girls Reds. Squad: Macey Sheard, Maddison Hirst, Jessica Woods, Cailin Carr, Jessica Harrap, Mia Simpson, Alliyha Rhodes, Allisha Rhodes, Elizabeth Grayson, Taylor Eccles, Caroline Maregere, Aome Stanley, Hermione Brown, Hannah Mullooly; Coaches: Wayne Hirst and Bridgette Woods.

Shaw Cross Under-10s 2017. Squad: Ross Cameron, Caitlin Cox, Louis Fisher, Oliver Gall, Charlie Hirst, Frankie Kilroy, Dylan Kindelan, Liam Littlewood, Jayke Kent, Billy March, Joshua Parkin, Jake Healey, Rowan Stephenson, Ellis Sykes, Finn Tartersfield, Liam Grundy, Ben Land, Luca Teal, Josh Whitworth, Harry Webster, Jessica Lumb, Alfie Lavery, Harry Wharton, Elliot Robson, Henry Dilley, Max Kaye, Luca Barraclough, Leona Salih, Caelan Calcutt, Samuel Busfield, Logan Murrell.

Shaw Cross Under-11s 2017. Squad: Andy Robinson, Ash Lindsay, Lewis Earnshaw, Reece Norman, Harry Hardwick, Louis Appleyard, Roco Parkin, Harri Lawn, Joe Wood, Tyler Parker, Lenni Laverick, Theo Robinson, Tylor Lindsay, Joel Webster, Harrison Lindsay, Archie Dufton, Kier Savage, Luke Maclaren, Tom Culling, Cameron Salih.

7. The Challenge Cup

As soon as the open age team was up and running the club started entering the RL Challenge Cup, although it never managed to progress beyond the qualifying rounds. A major revamp of the rules of the Challenge Cup competition saw 64 amateur clubs brought into the first round from 1993–94 onwards. That decision meant that the club, as members of the National Conference League, would be guaranteed a place in the Cup draw every year from then onwards.

Shaw Cross Sharks were part of that new wave and would be one of the early pace setters. While an amateur club does not realistically dream of reaching Wembley there is still the exciting prospect of reaching the third round, when members of the Second Division join the competition. Altogether Shaw Cross Sharks have reached that stage five times but have not so far been able to progress any further.

Although the Sharks were having a disappointing season in the National League, they passed the first hurdle in the Cup, beating Yorkshire League Fryston 12–6 to progress through to a meeting with Thatto Heath from the NW Counties League. A home victory, 11–4, put the Sharks into the third round. The Cup rules stipulated that third round ties must take place on the professional club's ground, so the draw sent the Sharks to north London to take on a London Crusaders' side that was very successful on the field, while struggling off it. A spell of bad weather meant that the Crusaders' home ground at Barnet was waterlogged and the match had to be played at the home of Hendon FC.

London Crusaders 40 Shaw Cross Sharks 14
16 January 1994 Attendance: 551

The Crusaders, who were being run largely by volunteers while under the RFL's financial control, were still vying for promotion from the Second Division. Under former New Zealand coach Tony Gordon, their squad had a strong New Zealand influence and featured big names like Londoner John Gallagher, a former All Black, and Sam Stewart, the Kiwi pack man. The Sharks scored first through a Simon Robertshaw penalty and he added a second before the interval, but it was clear that the Londoners had too much power and experience as they replied with five tries to make the score 24–4. After the break there was a spirited fight back by the Sharks, Richard Stephenson going over following clever work by Howard Marshall and Lee Roberts, before an interception by Daryl Bastow, converted by Graham Dobson, ended the scoring.

The Crusaders had comfortably beaten the Sharks 40–14 to progress through into the draw for the next round. Still, at least the Sharks had the consolation of collecting a £1,000 development grant for having reached the third round from the Silk Cut prize fund.

The following season's campaign began with a visit from the holders of the Southern Counties Cup, Fulham Travellers. A comfortable 46–20 victory saw the Sharks through to a meeting with fellow NCL member Moldgreen in the next round. Victory, 9–4, brought an almost perfect draw for the third round. The Sharks' next opponents were Batley, just a mile-and-a-half away on the opposite hill.

Batley 32 Shaw Cross Sharks 4

22 January 1995. Attendance: 1,126

Batley, doing well in the Second Division, provided strong opposition but Shaw Cross did have the satisfaction of recording the game's first try. Before Batley had even laid a finger on the ball Johnnie Ripley and Richard Gregory caught the home defence napping and sent Mark Chapman on his way to score. After that it was nearly all one way. A strong Batley team, destined to finish as Second Division runners-up, took control and monopolised the scoring to finish comfortable winners.

In December 1999, an easy first round victory over Townville from Castleford served up a more challenging tie against East Leeds to be played over the New Year's holiday weekend. The Sharks certainly appeared to have the more responsible team as they hammered the visitors 52–7 on the afternoon of the bank holiday Monday. The third round draw sent the Sharks on another long journey.

Whitehaven Warriors 42 Shaw Cross Sharks 0

30 January 2000. Attendance: 503

Bad weather seemed destined to make sure this match did not go ahead. By the time the team arrived on the Cumbrian coast on Saturday the Recreation Ground was flooded. By Sunday morning when the home chairman organised a pitch inspection it was under six inches of water and it looked certain the match would not go ahead. Believing that was the case, the supporters gathering at Shaw Cross for an early start for Cumbria were told not to travel. Having their plans for a long day out ruined, the supporters decided to make their own entertainment.

However, the local groundsman had said that he thought the ground would be alright once the tide went out and he was right. As if by magic, the flood disappeared and although the pitch was a quagmire the match went ahead. A huge Warriors' pack proving a handful and the Sharks' had to thank player-coach Deryck Fox's kicking game for pushing the home side back. But, by half-time the score was 30–0 and any chance of an upset had gone. After the break worsening pitch conditions and a committed Sharks defence restricted the home side to just two further converted tries, the second in the last minute. After a long journey home the team's bus arrived back at Shaw Cross to find a party in full swing.

For Whitehaven victory proved bitter sweet as two weeks later Wigan run up almost 100 points against them.

In December 2002, the draw for the first round paired the Sharks with Welsh opposition in the form of the Cardiff Demons. Such was the interest the match was switched to the nearby Dewsbury Rams' stadium. It was an uneven contest as the Sharks, already nearly halfway through their season, were too good for a Demons' team whose season had yet to start. The Sharks' won a one-sided match 56–12.

Two weeks later a trip to Oldham produced a good win, 18–4 over Waterhead. The third round draw brought another trip over the Pennines, this time to Moor Lane in Salford, the then home ground of Swinton Lions.

Swinton Lions 40 Shaw Cross Sharks 0
26 January 2003. Attendance: 315

The Lions scored in the fourth minute and were never really troubled after that. The Sharks produced a couple of breaks that nearly brought tries, but overall the professionals were just too powerful. Although it was a heavy defeat, the Sharks could take heart as the Lions battled through the next two rounds before losing to Wigan in the quarter-final.

In 2006, the start of the Cup campaign, which now began at the start of February, had brought a visit from Oldham St Anne's. A high scoring match was won by the Sharks 32–22. The second round saw the Sharks make the short journey over to Bramley in west Leeds where they beat the Buffaloes 28–22. This time the third round draw took the Sharks southwards to meet the newly named Doncaster Lakers, then playing at the old Rovers' football stadium at Belle Vue.

Doncaster Lakers 34 Shaw Cross Sharks 18
12 March 2006. Attendance: 545

The Lakers, members of National League One, were enjoying a promising start to the season and built up an early lead. The Sharks were playing well and thanks to a Danny Smith try were able to go in at the break only 18–4 down. After the interval the Sharks' rocked the Lakers with three tries – by Craig Lilley, Jamie Spence and Mick Colloby – to narrow the gap to just six points with 15 minutes left. Fearing an embarrassing defeat, the Lakers rallied to make the game safe.

Wayne and Darrel Bastow
with the Challenge Cup. They
both played against London
Crusaders in the 1994 match.

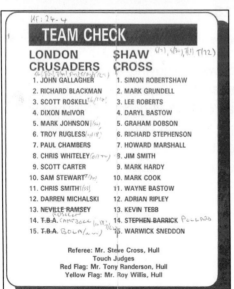

The teams from the programme for the 1994
Challenge Cup match away to London Broncos.

8. Coaches

Shaw Cross has always been fortunate in being able to call upon many former professional players to coach its teams. In the beginning it was Stan Gower, a former professional at Batley, who joined the club as rugby coach in 1952 and went on to become club leader five years later. He held that position until he retired in 1967.

The club has been fortunate that a number of its former playing members have returned to the club as coaches after a stint in the professional game. Gary Brook and Barry Robinson returned after spells with Halifax and Chris Squires after time spent with Dewsbury. Other locally based former professionals came to the club as junior coaches. Bernard Watson, who had played for Leeds and Bradford Northern, came back and coached the under-18s.

Deryck Fox came through the ranks at nearby St John Fisher before starting a very successful professional career with Featherstone Rovers (two spells), Bradford Bulls and Batley. Along the way Deryck made 14 appearances for Great Britain. His final year as a professional, 1998, was spent as player-coach at Rochdale Hornets, but at the end of that campaign he decided he had to call time on his playing career.

Wishing to stay involved in the game Deryck joined Shaw Cross for a two-year stint as player-coach around the Millennium. His arrival both raised the profile of the club and had an immediate impact on the field; the club nearly didn't lose a match for the rest of the season. Sadly, work commitments forced Deryck to resign in January 2002.

Photo: Deryck Fox playing for Featherstone Rovers. (Courtesy Robert Gate)

Four coaches look back

Gary Brook

Gary Brook came through the Wakefield junior ranks before embarking on a professional career with Doncaster, later moving on to Castleford and Halifax, before returning to Doncaster where he ended his playing days. After a short spell as Keighley's second team coach Gary agreed to take over the coaching duties at the Sharks: "I went to Shaw Cross in 1983–84 to be the first team coach. The team was quite young and at the end of the season we just avoided relegation.

The social club bar had just been opened, but the players after training wanted to go to the Crown pub after training. In my first match with Shaw Cross a player was injured and everybody said to me get on the field and treat the guy. I did not know it was my job to look after the injured players, but I gave it my best shot and learned very quickly.

The players had to buy their own strapping for injuries, so I got the lads to sell tickets every week, the profits went to buying medical supplies. The draw was at 10 o'clock on a Thursday so everybody stayed in the bar for the result,

The team was playing better and over the seasons we got promoted and won local cups.

In 1989 Shaw Cross entered the National Conference League. Our first away game was at Barrow Island. Quite a few of the players said they could not play because the coach was leaving at 9.30 in the morning and they could not make it. I made enquiries for the bus to stay at Skipton on the way back and most of the team went to Barrow Island. We stopped at Skipton every time we went to Cumbria for a few seasons. The bus got back to Shaw Cross for midnight

I was still coach when Shaw Cross first played a professional team. That was the London Crusaders in 1994. The lads did very well and the score was not very big."

Chris Smith

Chris first joined Shaw Cross in 1971–72 after playing initially at Batley Boys & Dewsbury Moor. He played in the under–17s, then under–19s and moved up to the first Open Age side until a knee injury put him out of action. Following surgery, Chris made a comeback with his local side Staincliffe before returning to the Sharks. He then took on the player–coach role with the 'A' team followed by three seasons coaching the NCL team.

After spells coaching Cleckheaton and Mirfield Chris returned to join the Open Age committee and was then elected to the executive committee. Chris was appointed chairman in 2005 and continued to coach juniors. He took an under–8s group through to under–18s, several of whom are now in the current Open Age squad.

He recalls: "I was in a dilemma once I decided to take on coaching duties as I still wanted to play but I knew my ability and fitness was on the wane at 36. I took on the 'A' team with Barry Robinson and we had a great time. Both Barry and I wanted to play, but we agreed to sub or watch depending on how many players we had each game.

Our top players were often drafted into the NCL team and this gave us an opportunity to put the boots on, but generally we were coaching from the touchline and we had a great spirit which reminded me of the times when I started playing.

Barry was a former top professional player with Halifax, but his simple 'get out there and knock seven bells out of them' team talk became legend at the club and believe me he did just that if he got on the field. Sadly, Barry passed away in 1995, aged 55, long before his time and he left everyone devastated by his loss. He will always be remembered for his infectious enthusiasm and commitment to his team and the club.

Eventually, Mel Tattersfield volunteered to help me with the 'A' team and he was another who like me hoped we had 17 players but would also put a shirt on. Mel was big on fitness and I liked the tactical side of Rugby League so together we blended well and became big friends outside the game. Together we took on the NCL coaching job when Gary Brook stood down due to business commitments. We knew the job was different as we had the pick of the club's players but we also knew some were more reliable and committed than others. Mel was black or white, he wanted to stick with the players who trained regularly and we agreed this was the right approach.

Initially we had a great team spirit and had a good run. The players knew the mentality and responded very well to get us in a great position for promotion to the Premier. We probably lacked strength in depth which cost us in the end but we had a great go at it the next season. We held our own but had to get used to the reality that many of our best players were also the busiest at work and we hardly ever had our strongest side together. We had some good cup runs reaching the quarter-final of the National Cup where we went down narrowly to Crosfields and lost in the Yorkshire Cup semi-final to a strong Hull Dockers team. After three seasons at the helm both Mel and I felt a change would benefit the club and we both stood down.

When playing or coaching and perhaps even more so when involved in administration it is important to have support from the people around you. I have been very fortunate to have that support from team mates, coaches and colleagues, but also importantly from my family and in particular my long-suffering wife Susan. She has worked alongside me helping to make things run smoothly. All the support from everyone has been sincerely appreciated."

Mick Turner

There can be few, if any, more dedicated to rugby league than Mick Turner. He has an insatiable appetite for the game and his energies for rugby have no boundaries. His life of rugby began at Shaw Cross Boys' Club when he joined as a junior player and soon became hooked on the game.

Apart from a short time with the Dewsbury Norths–Hanging Heaton side as an open age player and coach, Mick has spent most of his career at Shaw Cross Sharks.

He coached the under– 18s for three years and the Open Age side for nearly 15 years. He took the side to three Challenge Cup ties against Swinton, Batley and Doncaster. He now serves as chairman of the Open Age section.

Mick is an integral member of the club's executive committee and vice chairman of the club. He played a major role in the planning of the club's new building in 1998 and was responsible for organising and leading three open age club tours to Cape Town as well as tours to Serbia and the Czech Republic.

On top of that Mick has also found time to spend more than two decades with BARLA serving as national coach and international manager. He organised and travelled with many BARLA tours worldwide including Australia, Jamaica, Russia, South Africa, the South Pacific and Dubai. Mick has also a long association with the Heavy Woollen Amateur Rugby League and has served as chairman for more than 20 years.

"I have had some great times coaching Shaw Cross. In this period we played in the Challenge Cup against Batley, Swinton and Doncaster. We had some very good sides. When we got promoted to the premier division in 2004–05 we only dropped one league point all season. This team was captained by Ryan Halloran.

I coached the first team for 15 years and the under–18s for three seasons. I had a brief return coaching the winter team for a season and a half. In my time as coach I organised three tours to South Africa, one to Serbia and one to the Czech Republic.

I always surrounded myself with good people who I could not have managed without. I had some great assistant coaches in Chris Squires, Nigel Walsh and Lee Gilmour. In addition, I also had some very good 'A' team coaches and we would not have been as successful without them, namely Andy Scanlon, Kenny Tolson, Johnny Allott, Daz Senior, Richard Turner, Craig Simons and Daz Bastow. We also had the support of hard working committee people and some long serving kitchen staff, especially my wife Mandy.

We had a sprinkling of overseas players. Two of them have married and stayed over here – Brendan Murray who came in 1996 and Johnny Numa who came in 2004. We have had some Australian characters Jason Smith (Sword), Wayne Bruce (Batman), Mat Leo, Brett Pattinson (Pato), Trent Jordan, Jason Penny. We had Ty Fallon who played twice then signed for Featherstone Rovers and stayed about three seasons. My life, my friends, my work (Ravensport) and now my family all revolve around rugby league. All this starting from me playing rugby league at Shaw Cross at the age of 13."

Brett Turner

It is not surprising Brett would follow his father, Michael, to the Shaw Cross club. So many have done so and now we are seeing youngsters joining whose father and grandfather also played at the club.

Brett came along with his father one evening and joined the junior section. He was soon engulfed in rugby league game and it was not long before he was helping his dad with the training sessions. His playing career was relatively short before he decided to become a coach. Brett undertook coaching courses to become fully qualified and acted as an assistant coach before the opportunity came to take over as head coach for the National Conference side.

Over time Brett has become more and more involved in the club generally and is responsible for producing the match-day programmes as well as designing the club's shirts.

"I've spent the majority of my life in and around Shaw Cross club. I first joined as a six year old to play in the under–8s team. I flittered in and out of the game as a junior because, to be honest I was a terrible player, but as my father was first team coach from 1994 I was always in and around the club, whether I was running the water on, acting as touch judge or just supporting, I was there.

My first foray into coaching came as a 16 year old, and although I was probably too immature to take on such a position at the time, I knew that it was something that I wanted to do in the future. I have many great memories from my time as a coach at Shaw Cross.

One thing that really sticks out in my mind is the promotion winning season of 2013, when I worked alongside Joe Chandler. We had a fantastic team that year. They showed some great character to deal with losing arguably our best player in Ryan Glynn in the first few weeks of the season to a serious spinal injury that ended his playing career. It was a tough time for everyone at the club, but it galvanised our squad at the time and there wasn't a chance that we weren't getting promoted that year, narrowly missing out on winning the league title.

We had players such as Shaun Squires, Luke Blake, Salford Red Devils' recent signing Derrell Olpherts and Zach Johnson in the side that went on to play the game professionally the following season. These lads were complimented by club stalwarts Andrew Fawkes and John Rourke, future captain Danny Flowers and many other talented players in a strong squad.

In my time in charge I've been lucky to work with some fantastic players. Home grown lads like Sam Ottewell and Brandan French from the current team really stand out for me as gifted players, and we have people at the club like Alex Whittaker, who might not stand out so much on the field but had red amber and black coursing through his veins.

We've also been blessed with some cracking imports. Paul Adams, a free scoring Australian winger that was recommended by club president Mike Stephenson, Jake Dooner an outstanding second row forward that barely ever missed a tackle and of course the Byatt Brothers; Robbie and Matt, a classy centre and a prop forward that chewed up metres for fun. Monte Gaddis was our first ever American player at the beginning of the 2017 season, coming from Cleveland, Ohio and he worked harder than anyone I've seen and brought with him a fine pedigree in college football alongside bags of enthusiasm.

Left: Former first team coach and now club chairman Chris Smith.
Above: Former first team coach and now rugby chairman Mick Turner.

Mick Turner, Nigel Walsh and Alan Lancaster watch Douglas Hird laying
the foundation stone of the new clubhouse.

Alan Lancaster, Douglas Hird, Mike Stephenson and Dave Bradshaw.

Douglas Hird, Michelle Sullivan, Josh Pinder and Chris Smith. Joh was the first winner of the
Mick Sullivan Award.

I've coached at the club for 10 years at the time of writing this, and have had some ups-and-downs on the field. More ups than downs, but the one constant has been some good camaraderie and being surrounded by great friends. The job can be very tough at times, and unless you've done it you have no idea how much hard work goes on behind the scenes.

It's always been made infinitely easier for me by having the best secretary in the amateur game by my side in the form of Benny Richardson. A hard worker that's deservedly taken many a Clubman-of-the-Year honour home with him at the end of the season awards' night! I couldn't wish for a better administrator and he's worked some wonders when we've had players in front of the disciplinary too. The list of people that I've coached beside, David Hudson, Steve Jones, Andrew Fawkes, James Collins, Ryan Glynn and more is a list of people that I'll have friendships with for the rest of my life. Before this, from my playing days I met my closest friends, and it's true to say that all of my truly close friends are there as a result of this great club either directly or indirectly. I've travelled to France as a junior player three times and to Cape Town. None of this would have happened without the Shaw Cross club.

There are a lot of people out there, myself included that owe a great deal of thanks to Douglas Hird and his band of merry young men for making the brave decision to start this great club 70 years ago, and to the many volunteers that have carried on ever since. Thousands of unbreakable friendships have been made because of them and I thank each and every one of them for that from the bottom of my heart."

Officers in a league of their own

Douglas Hird BEM

Douglas was one of the founder members of the club in 1947 and was appointed as the founding secretary. When called up by the Army to do his National Service, Douglas stood down as secretary, but on his return resumed the position, which he still holds. He also served as club leader for many years.

For his work over the years Douglas was made a life member of the Heavy Woollen ARL and he was a founder member of the Yorkshire Junior ARL. He also served on the executive committee of the Yorkshire Association of Boys' Clubs for many years.

Besides rugby league, Dougie's other sporting interest has been skiing. He was a member of the Great Britain Journalists' ski-team in the Journalists World Championships held in Bavaria and Canada. He also took part in an Anglo-Norwegian trek on skis across the backbone of Norway, supported by a team of dogs and sledge.

Having started out as a junior reporter on the Saturday evening *Green Un* with the *Yorkshire Evening News*, Douglas built a career after National Service as a journalist with the *Batley Reporter* and the *Dewsbury Reporter*. He moved on to the *Bradford Telegraph and Argus* in 1957 where he worked for 31 years until his retirement. After 'retiring', he went freelance covering Dewsbury and Batley matches for the Press Association and various newspapers.

Many honours have come Douglas's way. He was awarded the BEM in the 1986 New Year Honours List for services to youth at Shaw Cross. After being inducted into the Rugby League Roll of Honour, he was nominated for a Torch Trophy, which is awarded for services to sport, by the RFL. The Duke of Kent presented the award to mark Douglas's 60 years of voluntary service to rugby league in December 2007.

As befits probably the longest serving administrator in any British sport he has been awarded a number of life memberships – the Yorkshire Junior League of which he is also President, the Heavy Woollen League, BARLA and of course the Shaw Cross club among them.

Alan Lancaster MBE
Alan enjoyed a long and distinguished association with this club. He was a founder member in 1947 and here he began his rugby career as a teenager, going on to serve the club in many capacities throughout his lifetime.

He developed into a very good scrum-half and was one of the first to move on from the club and play professionally, with Bradford Northern, Huddersfield and Doncaster. After becoming a father and starting a successful printing business, Alan returned to the club to coach the boys. He was greatly respected and soon became involved in the running of the club, being elected very quickly onto the management committee before becoming chairman. Finally, Alan became president, a position he would hold for many years with great pride and distinction.

In 1970, along with his friend and colleague Douglas Hird, Alan was joint founder of the annual Shaw Cross French Exchange programme with Villeneuve-sur-Lot. Nearly 2,000 young players have taken part in this very successful exchange which still continues every Easter and is the longest running exchange in rugby league.

In 1977 Alan and Douglas were joint managers of BARLA's under-18 pioneering tour to Australia and New Zealand which was the first ever tour 'down under' by an amateur British side.

Alan was awarded an MBE for services to young people in the Queen's New Year Honours List in 2008. It was an award he was humbled to receive, but richly deserved for he was a great believer in promoting opportunities for young people.

Alan was a long-serving executive member of the Yorkshire Association of Boys Clubs, later to become the Yorkshire Association of Clubs for Young People. He was also an active member of the Bradford Northern and Huddersfield past-players' associations. Sadly, Alan passed away aged 78 in May 2011.

Nigel Walsh
Nigel joined the club as a junior playing member at the age of 15 in 1974 and played until he was 34. He toured France in the exchange programme in 1978 as a player and returned in 1997 as coach to the under–16s squad alongside David Jackson.

Club Committee in the early 1990s. Back: Colin Roberts, Ken Ripley, Colin Stubley, Mick Bastow, Douglas Hird; front: Diane Broderick, Mavis Bastow, Alan Lancaster, Pam Broadhead, Heather Ainsworth, Mavis Woodcock.

Celebrating the Club's Golden Jubilee in 1997. Back: Douglas Hird, Alan Lancaster, Mary Stubley – Mayor of Kirklees, Kevin Millington, Gary Brook; front: Alan Smith, Stuart Broadhead, David Bradshaw, Ken Ripley. Long Service Awards were presented.

Prior to that he had joined the open age committee in 1992. Nigel became chairman of the club and the newly formed executive committee in 1995. He served on both the open age and the executive committee until 2010.

During this time he was also assistant coach to the under–18s and first team squads and worked with Mick Turner to organise the ground breaking tours to Cape Town and the trip to Serbia-Montenegro. His abiding memory is of 1998: "1998 was special. I was chairman of the club through the lottery grant bid, so the eventual opening of the new clubhouse and the winning of the sports club of Great Britain award made for a remarkable year.

It was a pleasure to take part in the running of the club in one of the most exciting and dynamic times in its history since its conception in 1947. To be able now to stand back and look at the new club house and the facilities and opportunities it gives to all young people of the area and to think I played a role in the securing the club's future is something I look back on with pride."

Clubmark Gold

The club achieved Sport England's Clubmark standard in 2004. The club officials were presented with the award at half-time during the Tri-Nations test between Great Britain and New Zealand at Huddersfield in November. As the first club in Dewsbury to achieve the award, the officials were keen to go on and achieve an even higher standard.

In 2010, thanks to the continued efforts of many volunteers, Shaw Cross was awarded Clubmark Gold. It was a proud moment for the club and reflected its achievement in being a well-managed club, striving to offer the best in coaching and sports development in a safe environment for children.

Alan Lancaster Award

The club is honoured to now present an annual award in the name of Alan Lancaster, who enjoyed a successful professional career before returning to put in years of service on behalf of the club. His family and the club wished to keep his memory alive with this prestigious award for a member who has given good service and is likely to continue that beyond their playing days.

There was no better inaugural winner than Andrew Fawkes who served the club as a player from a youngster through to open age and now continues as one of their senior coaches with the open age and under–14 girls' team in which Andy's daughter is a playing member. The club hopes that Andy will be an important part of the club's future going forward.

Mick Sullivan Award

Shaw Cross was very pleased to acknowledge the contribution of Mick Sullivan to the club when his daughter Michelle and his family donated this award in his name.

Mick's achievements are outlined elsewhere in this book. This award was set up for outstanding achievement on the field. The inaugural winner was Josh Pinder who was selected for England Under–16s and had also had an outstanding season with the Shaw Cross Under–16s. Josh was subsequently signed by Huddersfield Giants and the club wish him every success for his future following in Sully's footsteps to some degree.

The club has often supported charitable causes. The picture below is the Women's Committee, who played Churwell to raise money for Breast Cancer charities. Over £3,000 was raised.

Back: Mick Turner, Linda Hargill, Janice Boardman, Sandra Hirst, Tracy Grimwood, Lisa Chandler, Jan Shires, Susan Schofield, Mandy Turner; middle: Unknown, Jayne Drury, Linda Whittaker, Sandra Ellis, Mary Diskin, Michele Squires; front: Lesley Stones, Gill Day, Mandy Flowers, Hayden Turner, Unknown, Jenny Cawthron, Sally James , Debbie Annakin; very front: Jake Chandler.

Mick Turner, Gurdy Ryatt and Chris Smith. Gurdy played for the club as a junior and became the first Sikh to play professional rugby league, joining Hunslet in 1973–74. He later played several seasons for the Open Age side. He played second-row and was a popular team mate.

Shaw Cross Under–12s 2017. Squad: Max Sheard, Ben Andrassy, Bailey Ellis, Frazer Cass, Oliver Boocock, Nathan Smith, Joe McAllister Wood, Amir Kadir, Nathan Littlewood, Alex Baines, Josh Sanderson, Ewan Cameron, Oliver Bowie, Zak Yardley, Conor Bucknell, Josh Howgate, Harry Breakell, Thomas Power, Rhys Crookes, Callum McNaughton.

Shaw Cross Under–13s 2017 Squad: Callum Brian, Toby Calvert, Jamie Cox, Finley Curtis, Luke Etherington, Kian Fitzpatrick, William Gatus, William Hemingway, Freddie Lambert, James Lay, Ben Marsden, Luke Mearns, Breamar Murry, Finn Oxley-Szilagi, Spencer Peel, Oliver Robson, Evan Stephenson, Jude Senior, Jack Turton, Josh Wainwright, Bradley Wakenshaw, Ben Walker, Matthew Willert.

Shaw Cross Under–14s: Bulls squad 2017: Benjamin Aveyard, Nathan Barrett, Thomas Barrett, Josh Bathie, Josef Blythe, George Boot, Jackson Broadhead, Paul Chitakunye, Daniel Crawshaw, Myles Daly, Tobi Gardiner, Shae Hyland, Ryan Kelly, Liam Lewis, Logan Maddocks, Jacob Mort Firth, Joshua Oldroyd, Kieran Stoner, Sam Thompson, Fynnley Wilson. Sharks squad: Deacan Allen, Luke Barlow, Jaden Barraclough, Harris Brereton, Wesley Bruines, Mason Burgess, Jack Burton, Tyler Butterfield, Ethan Cox, Dylan Goodward, Oliver Grayson, Harrison Green, Taylor Hardwick, James King, Kian Lister, Callum Sykes, Rye Ward, Elliot Watson, Fynn Wilson, Arian Woods.

Shaw Cross Under–15s 2017. Squad: Harry Bowes (Captain), Elliott Richardson, Kobe Poaching, Elliott Butler, Reece O'Donnell, Luke Green, Tom Gibson, Robson Sutcliffe, Jack Audsley, Jack Oliver, Zak Crowther, Sol Devine, Sol Javidi, Harry Harvey, Harry Webster, George England, Oliver Farrar, Lewlyn McCormack, Ben Milner, Callum McGowan, Alfie Jackson, Josh Hayes.

9. Hall of Fame and more

In November 2011 Shaw Cross opened its Hall of Fame. A place in the Hall of Fame is awarded to all former players who have gone on to represent their country in a test or international match. An initial 15 former players were inducted: John Dalgreen, Nick Fozzard, Brian Gabbitas, Carl Gibson, Lee Gilmour, Tony Halmshaw, Douglas Hird, the late Alan Lancaster, Alan Redfearn, Dave Redfearn, David Smith, Mike Stephenson, Nigel Stephenson, Mick Sullivan, Derek Turner and David Ward.

John Dalgreen
Great Britain: 1982

John signed for Halifax in 1974, learning the game as he waited for his chance to make a first-team place his own. Before that happened he was transferred to Warrington in October 1977 where opportunities began to present themselves. Injury prevented John from making his debut for the Great Britain Under-24s in November 1979, but representative honours were only a matter of time. Needing a hooker to replace Tony Karalius, Fulham stepped in and signed John for £15,000 in August 1981.

His abrasive style rapidly made him a favourite with the Fulham fans. John became the Londoners' first test cap when he was called up to replace a fellow Shaw Cross product, David Ward, in the Great Britain team to face the 1982 Australians at Wigan's Central Park. A couple of years later, John rejoined Halifax in 1984 where he ended his playing career.

Nick Fozzard
Great Britain: 2005

As he looked to join the professional ranks, Nick Fozzard was in the enviable position of having half-a-dozen clubs chasing his signature. In the end he chose Leeds Rhinos, his father's old club. Nick's stand-out performances for the Rhinos led the Huddersfield Giants to pay out £90,000 for his services in 1997. Injury problems hampered his progress with the Giants and he moved on to Warrington Wolves in September 2001.

It was Nick's move to St Helens in 2004 that not only brought many club honours, but also international recognition. His club honours included winning the World Club Challenge and the Challenge Cup. He also played in the 2008 Grand Final, which St Helens lost to Leeds Rhinos. He was also selected for the 2007 Super League Dream Team.

He was called up by the Great Britain selectors for the 2005 Tri-Nations series and was chosen to play against New Zealand. He subsequently joined Hull KR for a year before returning to St Helens. He joined Castleford in 2010, and retired in 2012, following a shoulder injury. Overall, he made over 300 first team appearances.

Brian Gabbitas
Great Britain: 1959

Brian Gabbitas signed for Hunslet as a 16-year old in 1952–53. Called up into the Army, Alan impressed at rugby union and played for the Army team in 1953–54 and 1954–55. Once his National Service was over, Brian looked set for honours and was chosen for a tour trial match in 1958, but failed to make the squad. He was chosen to play for Great Britain against France in 1959, but that was his only cap. A one club man, Brian retired in 1965, shortly after sharing the Lance Todd Trophy for his performance against Wigan at Wembley in the Challenge Cup Final. He played 349 games for Hunslet over 14 seasons, and is a member of the club's Hall of Fame.

Carl Gibson
Great Britain: 1985 to 1991

Impressive performances at centre for Shaw Cross and Batley Boys under–18 team meant Carl Gibson had options when he considered turning professional. He stayed close to home and joined Batley in July 1981. Carl made a try scoring debut for the 'Gallant Youths' the following April. Such was his class that he was chosen for the Great Britain senior team, coming off the substitutes' bench against France at Headingley in March 1985. His cap was the first for a Batley player for 22 years.

In January 1986 Carl was transferred to Leeds for a £50,000 fee. Club honours at last came his way in a seven-year spell with the 'Loiners', with a Yorkshire Cup win in 1988. During his time at Headingley, Carl increased his tally of test caps to 11 and toured New Zealand and Papua New Guinea in 1990. Carl left Headingley in 1993 for a final two year spell with Featherstone Rovers before retiring.

Lee Gilmour
Great Britain: 1998 to 2006

A product of the Wigan Academy, Lee Gilmour was called up for the Great Britain squad that took on New Zealand in 1998. Perhaps because he could play either centre or second-row, Lee was often used as an impact player off the interchange bench. After a couple more years with Wigan, he moved on to Bradford where he was part of a very successful Bulls' squad. After the treble-winning success of 2003 Lee moved to the Bulls' main rivals, St Helens, and was part of their run of success that included the treble in 2006. Lee's test career, which had seen him make 15 appearances for Great Britain, drew to a close in 2006. He achieved other international honours. A Scottish grandparent resulted in a call up for Scotland in the 2000 World Cup tournament. He made three appearances. He left Saints at the end of 2009 and spent three years with Huddersfield Giants before moving nearer home with Castleford Tigers and Wakefield Trinity Wildcats. While still playing in Super League Lee came back to Shaw Cross to coach for a year before returning to play with the Sharks in mid-2016.

Tony Halmshaw
Great Britain: 1971

In 1964–65 Halifax signed a number of Shaw Cross players, but of them only Tony Halmshaw, who allegedly received a £1,000 signing-on fee, reached the highest level. Having appeared for England under-19s in 1964–65, Tony developed quickly in the Halifax 'A' team, and made a first-team place his own in 1968–69. His play for Halifax caught the selectors' eye and he was picked to play at loose-forward for Great Britain against New Zealand in November 1971. Unfortunately, Halifax were struggling to hold its own in the league and Tony was allowed to move on to Rochdale Hornets for £5,000 in March 1973. There was a further move, to Huddersfield, before Tony ended his playing career with his hometown club, Dewsbury, in the early 1980s.

Alan Redfearn
Great Britain: 1979

Alan followed his elder brother David to Bradford Northern in 1971 and made his first team debut four years later. It took him a little longer than his elder brother to establish himself in the first team, but once he did his strong tackling and incisive running from the base of the scrum made him a key component in Peter Fox's Championship winning team. His form brought selection for the 1979 Australasian tour and while down-under Alan made his test debut against Australia at the Sydney Cricket Ground. Upon his return he made the second of his two appearances for England in France in March 1980. There were no further international appearances for Alan, but he continued to play for Northern for another four seasons.

Dave Redfearn
Great Britain: 1972 to 1974

With an appearance for the England under–19s in 1969–70 it was no surprise that a number of professional clubs were chasing David's signature, but in the end he chose Bradford Northern when he turned professional in May 1970. A speedy try-scoring winger, Dave rapidly made his mark in the professional game and was selected for the 1972 World Cup in France, making his Great Britain debut against the host nation. As one of Britain's top wingers he toured Australasia in 1974.

His final international appearances were for England, the first against France in January and the last in a World Cup clash with Australia in November 1975. David enjoyed a long club career, all with Northern, where he played for nearly 20 years.

His playing days over, David followed up a number of opportunities before joining Sky Sports where he has worked for many years as a floor manager at Super League matches.

Above: John Dalgreen playing for Great Britain in 1982.
Right: Brian Gabbitas playing for Hunslet in the 1965
Challenge Cup Final. (Both photos courtesy Robert Gate)

Left: Carl Gibson
playing for Batley in
1983–84.
(Photo: courtesy *Rugby
League Journal*)

Right: Tony Halmshaw
(Photo: courtesy
Robert Gate)

Shaw Cross Under–11s in 1988–89. Lee Gilmour is the sixth player in from the left in the back row.

Shaw Cross Open Age teams around 1991–92. Back: Phil Sykes, Steve Naylor, Clive Gilbert, Richard Medley, Roger Toole, Mark Grundell, Gary Whittaker, Johnny Allot, Charlie Towey, Steve Barrick, Wayne Bastow, John Lumb; middle: Chris Smith(Coach), Simon Bailey, Richard Stephenson, Howard Marshall, Mark Hardy, John Agar, Ian Dalby, Dave Finnerty, Ady Ripley, Daz Render, Dave Walton, Andy Wood, Barry Robinson,(Coach), Gary Brook (Manager), Douglas Hird, Arthur Sedgwick Front, Mel Tattersfield (Coach) Richard Barker, Gary Pollard, Jonny Ripley, Steve Smith, Rob Hart, Steve Gower, Lee Roberts, Jeff Gilbert, Sean Moorhouse, Dale Holderness, Dave Hancock (Physio).

David Smith
Great Britain and England: 1975 to 1977

Originally a centre, David Smith was recruited by Wakefield Trinity and made a try-scoring first-team debut at the start of 1971–72. He followed that up that by equalling Trinity's try-scoring record two seasons later. Recognised as a match winning try-scoring winger, David played in the International Challenge Match against Australia in November 1975.

Having been targeted for some time, David was finally transferred to Leeds for £11,000, making his debut in the Lazenby Cup match in August 1976. Two try-scoring appearances for Great Britain under-24s against France caught the England selectors' attention and David was called up to play against France at Carcassonne in March 1977. Five years at Headingley was followed by an £18,000 move to Odsal where David spent another four seasons before hanging up his boots in 1985.

Mike Stephenson MBE
Great Britain: 1972 to 1974

Having left school, Mike Stephenson decided he wanted to take up rugby league again. Workmates encouraged him to join Shaw Cross and it proved to be a great choice. Benefitting from Dave Bradshaw's coaching, Mike made rapid progress through the ranks and this led him to join Dewsbury in 1966. Dewsbury was in the process of assembling a good team and Mike Stephenson was captain when they beat Leeds in the 1973 Championship Final. His outstanding performance in that final saw him awarded the Harry Sunderland Trophy as man-of-the-match.

Having played for the Great Britain under–24s against France in 1969, he made his debut off the bench against the Kiwis in 1971. By the time of Dewsbury's Championship win, Mike had appeared six times for Great Britain.

His mobile, play-making performances had not gone unnoticed in Australia. At the start of the 1973–74 season he was recruited by Penrith for a world record transfer fee of £20,000. In those days an Australian contract meant his test playing days were over, but Stevo nearly made history. With both hookers on the injured list, the 1974 Lions requested Stevo's services ahead of the second test in Sydney. He was keen to pull on the jersey again, but sadly the authorities ruled him out. Although there would be no more caps, Stevo went on to enjoy a successful playing career in Australia.

When his playing days were over Stevo spent 15 years as a journalist with the *Sydney Sun* before branching out into radio and television. At the start of the 1990s he grabbed the opportunity to start presenting rugby league on satellite television in Britain. When his original employer became part of Sky Sports, Stevo became an integral part of what became a longstanding team of presenters.

Nearer his old home, Stevo opened the Rugby League Heritage Centre at Huddersfield's George Hotel in 2005. He retained his links with Shaw Cross and succeeded Alan Lancaster as club President in 2011. He retired from the Sky Sports commentary team at the end of the 2016 season. Mike was awarded an MBE for his services to rugby league and broadcasting in the 2017 New Year's Honours List.

Nigel Stephenson
England: 1975

Dewsbury's signing of Nigel while still a 16-year-old schoolboy for a club record four-figure sum was considered sensational for a junior at the time. Unfortunately, an injury in an early 'A' team match meant Nigel did not make his first team debut until his second season as a professional in the 1967–68 season. He went on to gain major honours playing in a strong Dewsbury team. Nigel was called up by England selectors for the International Challenge Match against Australia which was held after the 1975 World Cup tournament had finished. Although he played for England it was unfortunate that the selectors had decided that no caps would be awarded. His other representative honours were for Yorkshire with 10 appearances.

Nigel moved on to Bradford Northern in November 1978 where a change of position from centre to stand-off brought further medals, but no further representative honours. By now at the veteran stage Nigel was signed by the newly Carlisle Border Raiders for £20,000 in 1981. A year later Nigel was on his way again, signing for Wakefield Trinity for a £25,000 fee. Nigel spent two seasons at Belle Vue before returning to Dewsbury. He then played for York from 1986 to 1988. His playing days over, Nigel became a member of Peter Fox's coaching staff at Odsal in the early 1990s.

Mick Sullivan
Great Britain: 1954 to 1963

Mick Sullivan was Shaw Cross's first star player. After appearing for the England open age amateur and Under–19 teams, Sully received £500 when he was signed aged 18 by Huddersfield in May 1952. Sully made rapid progress in the professional game and was a surprise choice by the Great Britain selectors for the 1954 World Cup tournament in France. He returned from France with an enhanced reputation which was boosted further by his displays for the RAF rugby union team during his National Service.

After handing in his uniform he was twice the subject of record transfer deals as he moved from Huddersfield to Wigan and then Wigan to St Helens, collecting numerous honours along the way.

Having taken over the left wing jersey in the 1954 World Cup tournament, Sully held onto it for the best part of a decade. By the time he collected his last Great Britain cap in November 1963, he had made 46 appearances, a record number which has been equalled, but will almost certainly never be beaten. During his record run for the Lions, Sully also appeared three times for England. What was remarkable about those appearances was that he made the first two of them against France and Other Nationalities in 1955–56 before the team was mothballed. When the England team resurfaced in November 1962 Sully was chosen thereby retaining his place after a gap of six years.

Although time might have been called on his test career, Sully enjoyed a brief but glorious spell as player-coach with Dewsbury that so nearly ended with a visit to Wembley in 1966.

Coaching beckoned, including some time spent in Australia, but after a couple of short unsuccessful appointments he ended his professional connection with the game. Sully remained a loyal supporter of Shaw Cross, regularly attending the club's functions and events right up until the onset of his final illness.

Derek Turner
Great Britain: 1956 to 1962

After a spell playing for Ossett RUFC, Derek switched codes and joined Hull KR aged 18, making his debut at loose forward in September 1951. A few matches followed as a centre before Derek made a pack place his own. A born leader, he moved on to Oldham for a transfer fee of £2,750 in 1955. His time at Watersheddings was disrupted by the need to complete his National Service. Impressing in a strong Oldham pack, Derek made his Great Britain debut against the Australians in 1956. His play was attracting attention and Wakefield Trinity splashed out a club record fee of £8,000 to sign him in March 1959.

By the time he finally retired in August 1966, 'Rocky' had gained every club honour available to a player. He had accumulated 24 caps Great Britain caps, two of them when he captained the Lions in both tests in New Zealand in 1962. He had also appeared once for England against France in 1962.

His playing days over, Derek enjoyed a successful coaching career, first spending three seasons with Castleford before in the summer of 1969 moving on to Leeds where he spent three equally successful seasons. Derek's coaching career finally ended after a short spell with Wakefield Trinity in the 1980s.

David Ward
Great Britain and England 1977 to 1982

His schooldays in Wakefield over, David joined Shaw Cross and it was from there that the 17-year old signed for Leeds in May 1971, making his professional debut at the start of the following season. It was to be the start of a long and successful career at Headingley. Many club honours had come his way before the selectors recognised David's qualities as a ball-winning hooker. An appearance for the Great

Britain under–24 team was followed by selection for the 1977 World Cup tournament.

At this time the RFL was regularly fielding an England team and David made six appearances for his country between 1977 and 1981. Having made his Great Britain debut out in Australia, David regularly occupied the hooker shirt and against France in 1981 he became the second Shaw Cross product to captain the Lions. David's second outing as captain unfortunately coincided with his final test appearance. Hull FC's Boothferry Park ground on the last Saturday in October 1982 was an unhappy day for British Rugby League as the all-conquering Australians won 40–4.

David's playing career lasted for 15 years at Headingley, during which time he led the Loiners to many honours. He made 482 appearances for Leeds, scoring 40 tries, two goals and 15 drop-goals.

His playing days ending abruptly when he announced he was retiring to take over as coach at Hunslet in 1986.

His coaching career developed at Hunslet. They won the Second Division in his first season in charge, but they were relegated the following season and he left the club. After a short spell playing for Workington, in 1989 he returned to Headingley as Malcolm Reilly's assistant. When Reilly quit early in 1989–90, David was appointed as head coach, a position he held until the arrival of Doug Laughton in 1991 prompted him to resign. After that, David moved to Batley, where he coached for almost a decade.

The Welsh connection: Jordan James
Wales 2003 to 2013

Bath born Jordan James developed an interest in rugby league while serving in the Royal Marines. Having started out with Gloucestershire Warriors, Jordan moved north after leaving the Marines and after a spell with Rotherham joined Shaw Cross before turning professional with Sheffield Eagles in mid-2003. His career spanned a dozen years, and was mostly spent in Super League.

He played for Castleford Tigers, Wigan Warriors, Widnes Vikings, Celtic Crusaders and Salford City Reds. He also played in the National League with South Wales Scorpions, Workington Town and Swinton Lions before retiring in 2015 to turn to coaching.

Jordan's Welsh connections were brought to the attention of the Wales selectors and lead to a remarkable 2003 season for him. After he made his last appearance for Shaw Cross, Jordan signed for Sheffield Eagles, played for them in the League One Qualifying Final and was then called up to make his international debut for Wales against Russia a fortnight later.

A decade later Jordan made his 30th and last appearance for Wales against the Cook Islands in the 2013 World Cup.

Left: Alan Redfearn. Right: David Redfearn.
(Both photos courtesy Robert Gate)

David Smith scoring in the Challenge Cup Final at Wembley for Leeds in 1978.
(Photo: Courtesy *Rugby League Journal*)

Mike Stephenson scoring for Dewsbury in the 1973 Championship Final.
Below: Left: Nigel Stephenson; Right: Derek Turner. (Both photos courtesy Robert Gate)

Mick Sullivan tangling with Tom van Vollenhoven. (Photo: courtesy Robert Gate)

David Ward. (Photo: Courtesy Robert Gate)

Keith Mason junior
Wales: 2001 to 2002

Dewsbury-born prop Keith Mason played for Shaw Cross and Dewsbury Moor before signing for Wakefield Trinity Wildcats just prior to the Millennium. There was Welsh blood in his family and that enabled Mason to get a call up for the Welsh team that met England in July 2001. Still in his early twenties, Mason moved to Australia at the start of 2002, signing for Melbourne Storm. He became the youngest British player to play in the NRL and represented Wales against New Zealand in November 2002. Mason returned to England in mid-2003 and joined St Helens where he gained major club honours. After the Saints Keith played on with Castleford and Huddersfield until 2013 when he became a movie actor.

A famous physio – Dave Hancock

In the late 1990s the club had a great physio called Dave Hancock who was based at Pinderfields Hospital in Wakefield for the final year of his Chartered Physiotherapist Degree. All the players knew he was something special which was borne out by his later roles as a head physio at Wolverhampton Wanderers, Blackburn Rovers, Leeds United, Chelsea FC, England and New York Knicks. He just turned up at the club looking for experience of treating sports injuries and went on to such heights. He is currently Chief Executive Officer and founder of Atherapy who have clinics in the UK and USA. Dave is now based in Manhattan.

Modern media
Shaw Cross's first experience with modern media began with James Stott. James had played for the juniors and youth teams, but suffered a bad shoulder injury which curtailed his playing career. He decided to make a positive contribution to the club by becoming its programme editor and website developer. He created the club's first website and it went on to win Website of the Year from the NCL thanks to his hard work.

James's father Andy has been a long serving player and committee member and between them they contribute to the club's fantastic matchday programme, one of the best in the NCL.

James also became adept at match reporting covered local professional games for the rugby league press. His hard work was rewarded with a national award as Young Achiever of the Year due to his determination to contribute to the club's success when his playing career was no longer an option. James went to London with chairman Chris Smith to receive this prestigious award which was thoroughly deserved. When his career in banking took off and his family life made time limited he passed the baton to Ryan Conway who took the club's media onto Twitter, Facebook and YouTube. He did a great job before going into a full-time media career.

The club's current media manager, Ben McKenna, also keeps Shaw Cross in the spotlight with frequent matchday tweets, regular website updates and some great match reports in the local press. The common denominator for all the media guys is their love of the club and enthusiasm for the game of rugby league.

Alan Smith

Now nearly 20 years old, the Shaw Cross Social Club continues to play an important role in both the game and the local community. In addition to the Sharks the club serves as the headquarters for the Heavy Woollen District ARL and the Yorkshire Junior ARL. It is also the regular meeting venue for the Yorkshire Men's League.

For the local community, the social club provides a place for a drink on a weekday evening or at the weekend. It also provides a function room where all sorts of celebrations, commemorations and get-togethers can be held.

Today the social club is managed by Alan Smith. His long association with Shaw Cross Sharks began 27 years ago when he brought his seven year old son, Danny to the club. He remembers the old club building when they started children's discos, which were very popular at the time, and the annual bonfires which were one of the highlights of the year. Danny progressed through the rugby league age groups to Open Age and was selected for the BARLA tour to South Africa in 2007 before joining Wakefield Trinity.

In the meantime, Alan became involved in coaching at the club and qualified as a referee for the Dewsbury and Batley Referees' Society. Alan continued coaching up to 2015 and also served on the junior committee before being appointed secretary. He has also served as chairman.

Alan is very involved with the club's French Exchange and following the retirement of the founders Douglas Hird and Alan Lancaster, he and Tracy Grimwood took over the organisation of the tours.

Shaw Cross Under–16s 2017. Squad: Harrison Sutcliffe, Edward Joyce, Ben Tibbs, Billy Aveyard, Will Clarke, Connor Bailey, Ryan Sedgewick, Eion Bowie, Cameron Lees, Adam Moore, Bailey Barker, Brad Baines, Harrison van der Wal, Callum Burden, Alfie Brown, Jamie Greenhall, Charlie Blockley, Wojciech Drop, Lewis Ashcroft, Hugo Lescouzeres, Tom Danson. Coach: Simon Bailey; Assistant coach: John Clark; Manager: Lee Tibbs; Doctor: Richard Sedgewick.

Shaw Cross Under–18s 2017. Jamie Hartley, Levon Heaps, Will Heywood, Ethan Ellis, Callum Barker, Jack Earnshaw, Tennison Neagle, Elliot Schofield, Dan Cass, George Stones, Tom Murphy, Kayne Tyrell, Tom Markland, Joe Thresh, James Sutherland, Brandon Warrior, Jack Gilbert, Tyrone Mashing Was. Coaches: Matt Cawthron, Dean Heywood; Touchline: Stephen Barker; Team secretary: Christine Speight; Coaches Assistant: Ernie Earnshaw.

10. Other sports

Although the club is best known for its success in the world of rugby league, it has over the years organised other sporting activities and taken part in various local competitions. Today, no other sections operate, but it is good to remember the days when the following sports were alive and kicking at the club.

Angling
An angling section was run for a few years. During that time Reece Broadbent won the NABC national competition when it was held at Doncaster.

Chess
In 1968 Roy Hampshire was presented with the YABC County Colours for Chess. He went on to win the County Chess title in the YABC championships, the first member to achieve that honour. His success led to him being chosen by the YABC to represent the county in the NABC championships in London. Roy would go on to repeat his success in 1971–72.

Association football
Bill Airey junior and his friends wanted to play association football, but there was no opportunity for them at their age in the Shaw Cross area. With the Boys' club on their doorstep Bill Airey's dad, Bill Airey senior, approached the club and it was agreed a new section would be formed. Bill Airey senior took charge and the football section got underway in 1960.

Enough players were gathered for a team to be entered into the Heavy Woollen Minor Under–18 League. As the decade progressed the club entered the Ossett and District Youth League and later the West Yorkshire League. The team made a superb debut in the West Yorkshire League becoming champions and challenge cup winners of Division Three North at the first attempt in 1967–68. Two years later the senior team won promotion to Division One of the West Yorkshire League. Eventually two teams were being run.

The 1970s were enlivened by some international visitors. The first visitors were invited over by the football section, in conjunction with the YABC, which was pioneering links with the Hamm area of what was then West Germany. The visit went well and touring parties were sent over to Germany and return visits were welcomed to Dewsbury. Next came some visitors from an unexpected source, Dallas, Texas. They were known as the Texas Longhorns. Made up of three youth teams, the Longhorns played matches on the three Grange Road pitches simultaneously. Although not very good at the game, their visit proved to be very entertaining.

A number of players went on to sign for professional forms. Most were local – like Bill Airey junior and Peter Ginnelly signing for Huddersfield Town and John Murgatroyd for Halifax Town but others went further afield, like Shaun Dunford who signed for Chelsea before returning home to play rugby league as a goalkicking winger for Dewsbury.

Bill Airey senior lived opposite the club pitches on Leeds Road, and it was there, in his front garden, that the goal posts and nets were stored between matches. It was his team's first duty on match day to carry the posts and nets over the road and to take them back after the final whistle. Bill remained in charge right up until his untimely death in 1982. His loss dealt a severe blow to the section from which it could not recover and it disbanded never to be re-formed.

Swimming

In the 1960s a swimming section was formed and the club became keen participants in the Dewsbury Youth Organisations Swimming (Boys') Trophy competition, winning it on several occasions. A number of members went on to win County Swimming Badges.

The section had its most successful in 1969–70, winning both the Dewsbury and YABC trophies. Success in the YABC championships led to the Shaw Cross team being selected to represent the county in the national swimming championships held at Crystal Palace where Malcolm Barnsley won the 220 yards freestyle event.

Table tennis

In the early 1970s the game was very popular and two teams were entered into the Dewsbury Red Triangle Table Tennis League. The section lasted for many years, but like the competitions it entered is long gone.

Playing the round ball game: Shaw Cross Association Football team 1967. Back: Billy Airey, John Murgatroyd, Gary Blakeley, David Hargreaves, Barrie Horsley, Geoff Wilson, Bill Airey (Coach); front: Roy Carter, Kenny Walton, George Wilson, Trevor Haldenby, Stuart Green.

Shaw Cross Association Football team on tour to Hamm in West Germany in 1976.

Masters rugby league has developed in recent years as a way of keeping older players involed in the sport. Shaw Cross Touch Team: Back: Aidy Ripley, Danny Scargill, John Lumb, Jonny Numa, Daz Senior, Brendan Murray, Rob Hinchcliffe; Front: Mark Land, Roger Toole, Lee Roberts, Richard Stephenson, Chris Squires, Chris Smith.

11. 70 years on and still reaching forward

There is only one way that this celebration of the first seventy years of Shaw Cross and that is by looking forward to the next milestone and even the one after that. The job of providing the final words fall to club chairman Chris Smith: "To reach a milestone of 70 years is a tremendous achievement for any club and we must give our respect and admiration for the efforts of our predecessors for creating such a great legacy for the game.

However, 70 is just a milestone and we march onwards and in keeping with the club motto we must continue 'Reaching Forward'. We are fortunate to have a fantastic group of coaches and volunteers who are enthusiastic, energetic and committed. Our future will rely on many of these people moving in to the management of the club in years to come.

The quality of people we have within the club gives us confidence that the legacy will continue and new chapters in our history will be created in the coming years. In that time thousands more youngsters will pass through our doors and be enriched by the experience of making new friends, enjoying the best sport in the world and broadening their horizons. Many will excel and progress to professional levels while many more will simply find that being involved with Shaw Cross is such a great foundation for their lives ahead.

We know today that while our facilities are good in comparison to many, they are close to capacity with the increasing demand we see. The area's population is growing and we have to look at expanding the facilities now to cater for the future. We have plans to add additional changing rooms that are desperately needed and are working to determine the best solution for this. There is land adjacent to the club which is currently derelict and the acquisition of this site would allow us to create the expansion we surely will need if we are to serve the growing community around us. This ideal solution is one of several options to consider and we will be working hard towards this goal.

As mentioned earlier, we have enjoyed an exchange with France for nearly 50 years. The first exchange took place in 1970 and we still have strong connections with the Villenueve & Tonniens junior clubs which will ensure the exchange continues to enrich the lives of the young players who participate. We have also discussed the idea of our senior players touring having had several successful tours in the past when we have taken the game to developing areas. It is time to give thought to our next adventure abroad.

Our club has always been recognised as one of the best in the junior and amateur game and it is our intention to continue working hard to maintain that great reputation. Our senior side play in the flagship National Conference League and have done so for many years. We have a senior side in the Yorkshire Men's League full of

James Stott and Chris Smith at the Young Achiever of the Year Awards in 2011.

young players which gives us great hopes for the future. Currently we have 15 junior teams which include our girl's teams and we are running rugby tots for those too young to play. The future is bright and we now have the challenge of advancing the club to ensure that we have the facilities and infrastructure to welcome all new players who want to experience what Shaw Cross has to offer."

Appendix 1: Shaw Cross Club for Young People

Honorary Vice-Presidents
J. Lyttle
J.D Matthewman
T. Scargill

Honorary Life Members
D.M. Hird BEM
M.A. Turner
J.D. Ellison
A. Lancaster MBE
P. Haselgrave
S. Broadhead
K. Fisher
K. Ripley
M. Hirst
G. Brook
A. Stott
A. Smith
D. Bradshaw
S.H. Gower
K. Millington
N. Walsh
M. Stephenson MBE
E. Firth

B. Clarke
J. Burland
R.H. Cropper
C. Squires
T. Grimwood
C. Stubley
K. Squires
S. Jones
B. Robinson
J. Kershaw
A. Myers
C. Smith
A. Ripley
L. Chandler
D. Ellis
D. Bastow

Life Members
D. Dyson
B. Carter
G. Squires
J. Fort
A. Dauriac
J. Salisbury

Appendix 2: Players who became professionals

Members who became professional rugby league players and the clubs they joined.

Brad Adams: Bradford, Dewsbury
Jamaine Akaidere: Huddersfield, Dewsbury, Hunslet
Chris Annakin: Wakefield
Danny Annakin: Dewsbury
Peter Armstead: Batley, Wakefield
Peter Barlow: Wakefield, Bramley
Trevor Barlow: Batley
Michael Basten: Dewsbury
Stan Beaumont: Castleford
Melvyn Bedford: Dewsbury, Batley
Trevor Bedford: Dewsbury, Castleford
Graham Bell: Dewsbury
John Bell: Wakefield Trinity, Castleford
Alan Bence: Leeds, Wigan, Castleford
Michael Berry: Halifax
Ged Birkin: Halifax
Peter Blackburn: Dewsbury
Keith Boocock: Dewsbury
Stephen Booth: Halifax
Roy Borthwick: Halifax
Gerald Brentnall: Batley
Declan Bretherton: Dewsbury
David Briggs: Dewsbury
David Brooke: Batley
Stephen Brown: Halifax
David Busfield: Featherstone Rovers, Halifax, Hull, Wakefield, Dewsbury
Stuart Butcher: Dewsbury
Ian Butterfield: Dewsbury
Donald Callender: Huddersfield
Will Carlos: Huddersfield
John Carroll: Leeds, Batley, Hull, Halifax
Dan Cass: Huddersfield Giants
Geoffrey Catlin: Dewsbury
Joe Chandler: Leeds, Halifax, Batley, Oldham, Keighley
Jeffrey Chappell: Dewsbury
John Clark: Doncaster, Huddersfield
John Clark: Dewsbury
Tom Colleran: Dewsbury
Will Colleran: Wakefield
Michael Colloby: Halifax
Matthew Colloby: Bradford
Mark Cook: Mansfield, Batley

Barrie Cooper: Halifax, Hull KR
Alan Craven: Batley, Dewsbury
Tony Crew: Dewsbury
John Croft: Bradford Northern
John Dalgreen: Halifax, Warrington, Fulham
James Davies: Bradford Bulls
Trevor Davies: Dewsbury
Kevin Dickens: Oxford
Steven Dickens: Leeds, Salford, Keighley
Chris Dobbs: Halifax
Neil Dobson: Doncaster
Peter Dransfield: Halifax, Batley
Shaun Dunford: Dewsbury
Joseph Durkin: Huddersfield
David Dyson: Halifax, Bradford N
Frank Eastwood: Featherstone R
Alan Edwards: Keighley, Dewsbury
Jack Farrar: Dewsbury
Andrew Fawkes: Dewsbury
Brian Field: Halifax
David Finnerty: Halifax, Doncaster
Max Fletcher: Dewsbury
Jack Flynn: Huddersfield Giants
Frank Fox: Halifax, Hull KR, Castleford
Nick Fozzard: Leeds, Huddersfield, Warrington, St. Helens, Hull KR, Castleford
Peter Fozzard: Leeds
Peter Frain: Keighley
John Frain: Dewsbury
Michael Frain: Halifax
Brian Gabbitas: Hunslet
Tommy Gallagher: Leeds, London B, Widnes, Toulouse, Hull KR, Batley, Swinton, Leigh, Dewsbury.
Leslie Gant: Bradford Northern
David Garforth: Dewsbury
Peter Garner: Dewsbury
Michael Gibson: Keighley
Carl Gibson: Batley, Leeds, Featherstone
Lee Gilmour: Wigan, St Helens, Huddersfield, Castleford, Wakefield
Ben Gledhill: Wakefield, Salford
Ryan Glynn: Dewsbury
George Goodyear: Doncaster
Trevor Gower: Dewsbury

Robert Gowan: Huddersfield
Kenneth Grace: Keighley
Richard Gregory: Hunslet
Tom Griffiths: Wakefield
Stephen Grinhaff: Halifax, Batley, Bramley
Gary Hale: Wakefield Trinity, Bradford Northern
Leslie Hall: Batley
Stuart Hall: Doncaster
Stephen Halloran: Halifax, Dewsbury
Tony Halmshaw: Halifax
Brian Hardcastle: Halifax, Keighley
Michael Harris: Dewsbury
Brian Harrison: Batley
Tony Hastelow: Huddersfield
Stanley Helliwell: Dewsbury
Jack Hemmins: Batley
David Heppleston: Huddersfield
Ryan Hepworth: Sheffield, Dewsbury
Tony Hepworth: Halifax
Keith Hepworth: Dewsbury
Trevor Hobson: Dewsbury
Peter Hodgson: Doncaster
James Hopwood: Batley
Richard Hoyle: Dewsbury
George Hutchinson: Dewsbury, Featherstone Rovers
Kenneth Huxley: Hull
Richard Ineson: Bradford Northern
Stanley Jackson: Dewsbury
Jordan James: Wigan, Crusaders, South Wales, Swinton, Widnes, Castleford, Sheffield Eagles, Salford
Zac Johnson: Dewsbury, Swinton, Coventry Bears
Alan Kane: Huddersfield
Stuart Kelley: Halifax
Abdul Khan: Bradford
Austin Kilroy: Batley, Huddersfield
Alan Lancaster: Bradford N, Huddersfield
Tony Laycock: Dewsbury
Scott Lee: Leeds, Wakefield, Keighley
Ashley Lindsay: Dewsbury, Batley, Keighley
Allen Lockwood: Dewsbury, Hull KR, Leeds
Peter Lovell: Batley
Trevor Lowe: Dewsbury
Timothy Lumb: Hunslet, Sheffield
Ronnie Lyles: Castleford
John Maloney: Hull
Douglas Manners: Dewsbury, Batley

Leslie Marriott: Dewsbury
Geoffrey Marsh: Dewsbury
Keith Mason junior: Wakefield, Melbourne Storm, St Helens, Huddersfield, Castleford
James Masson: Doncaster
John McGowan: Batley
Colin Midgley: Dewsbury
Hayden Mitchell: Featherstone Rovers, Dewsbury
Jack Mitchell: Huddersfield
Robert Mitchell: Huddersfield
David Mordue: Bradford N
Philip Morgan: Halifax
Stanley Moyser: Batley, Dewsbury, Halifax, Hunslet
Ian Muir: Huddersfield
Peter Mullins: Dewsbury, Bradford
Curtis Naughton: Hull, Bradford, Leigh
Danny Naughton: Huddersfield
James Naylor: Dewsbury
George Newsome: Dewsbury
Jeffrey Newton: Halifax
Robert Nicholson: Dewsbury
Paul O'Hara: Halifax
Peter Oldroyd: Rochdale Hornets
Derrell Olpherts: Dewsbury, Hemel Hempstead, Newcastle, Salford
Kevin Osborne: Dewsbury
Clive Page: Dewsbury
Melvyn Page: Wakefield Trinity
Andrew Parkinson: Halifax, Batley
David Peace: Blackpool Borough
Gary Pearson: Hull
Brandon Pickersgill: Bradford Bulls, London Skolars
Jos Pinder: Huddersfield Giants
Graham Pitchforth: Halifax
Jay Pitts: Leeds, Wakefield, Hull, Bradford, London Broncos
Zygmunt Piwinski: Batley, York
Luke Powell: Wakefield
Richard Price: Hull, Sheffield, Batley
David Redfearn: Bradford N
Alan Redfearn: Bradford N
Trevor Rhodes: Doncaster, Batley
Adrian Ripley: Wakefield
Barrie Robinson: Halifax
Brian Robinson: Dewsbury
Paul Robinson: Dewsbury
Philip Robinson: Dewsbury

John Rourke: Batley
Gurdeep Ryatt: Hunslet
Kevin Scanlan: Dewsbury
Andrew Scanlan: Keighley
Bernard Scott: Halifax, Swinton
Alan Seeling: Keighley
David Senior: Batley
Robert Senior: Bradford
Edward Sharp: Batley, Wakefield
Ian Sharpe: Dewsbury
David Shaw: Halifax
Colin Shires: Halifax
Andrew Smith: Keighley
Bernard Smith: Batley
Danny Smith: Wakefield, Huddersfield
David Smith: Halifax
David 'Ginger' Smith: Keighley
David Smith: Wakefield, Leeds
Joe Smith: Keighley
Paul Smith: Keighley
Michael Snee: Halifax
Walter Spurr: Dewsbury
Shaun Squires: Sheffield Eagles, Batley, Dewsbury
Graham Standidge: Hunslet, Batley
Mike Stephenson: Dewsbury, Penrith (Sydney)
Nigel Stephenson: Dewsbury, Bradford Northern, Carlisle, Wakefield, York
Trevor Stephenson: Halifax
Mike Stewart: Gloucester, Hemel Hempstead
Michael Sullivan: Huddersfield, Wigan, St Helens, York, Dewsbury
Graham Summerscales: Dewsbury

Martin Summerscales: Dewsbury
Philip Sunderland: Leeds
Liam Sutcliffe: Leeds, Bradford
Gordon Talbot: Dewsbury
Brian Taylor: Dewsbury, Batley
Matthew Tebb: Dewsbury, Hunslet
Andrew Tillotson: Dewsbury
Keith Toohey: Batley, Bradford N
Glen Towey: Halifax
Arthur Townend: Featherstone Rovers, Doncaster
Robert Tucker: Keighley
Barry Turnbull: Dewsbury
Derek Turner: Hull KR, Oldham, Wakefield
Norman Wainwright: Huddersfield, Batley
Vic Wainwright: Halifax
Bernard Walker: Dewsbury
Pat Walker: Dewsbury, Sheffield, Batley
Robert Walker: Dewsbury
Trevor Walker: Dewsbury, Batley
David Walton: Halifax
David Ward: Leeds
Gordon Waring: Dewsbury
Malcolm Waring: Dewsbury, Keighley
Philip Watts: Batley
Robert Whiteford: Batley
Barrie Whittaker: Batley
Joseph Whittington: DewsburyDavid Wilmot: Keighley
Clive Wisher: Dewsbury
James Wood: Dewsbury
Stuart Wood: Dewsbury
Darryl Woollin: Halifax
Robert Young: Doncaster

Appendix 3: BARLA Representatives

Great Britain Open Age
Graham Smith, Jimmy Wood, Gary Shaw, John McGowan, Graham Summerscales, Johnny Ripley, Danny Smith, Mathew Myers, Ash Lindsey, Pat Foulstone, John Rourke, Zach Johnson, Shaun Squires.

Great Britain Under–17s, Under–19s, Under–-21s, Under-23s
Andrew Fawkes, Richard Squires, Brandan French, Lee Gilmour, Sam Ottewell. Steve Talbot, Craig Lilley, Stephen Shaw, Danny Rowse, Adam Masson, Casey Johnson, Joe Halloran, Will Gaunt, Patrick Walker, Chris Jones, Reece Parker, Tom Wall, Ash Lindsey, Pat Foulstone, John Rourke, Zach Johnson, Martyn Holland.

Great Britain Over–35s Tourists
Johnny Numa, Andy Burland, Kevin Dickens, Wayne Hirst,

Great Britain Managers
Mick Turner: Open age, Under–21s, Under–23s, Over–35s
Douglas Hird, Alan Lancaster: Under–18s
Graham Parker: Under–17s

Coaches
Mick Turner: Open Age, Under–21s, Under–23s
Brett Turner: Under–17s

Physios
Terry Palfaman, Gordon Gray Cowan, Richard Sedgewick, Rob Stephenson.

Equipment Managers
Steve Jones, Pat Cox: Open Age.
Kevin Squires: South Pacific tour 2011
James Stephenson: Under–17s

Conditioners
Chris Squires: Over–35s
David Hudson: Under–17s

Appendix 4: Statistics and records

Dewsbury & Batley Amateur Rugby League / Heavy Woollen ARL

Division Two (Open Age): Champions 1979–80

Jim Brown Cup: Winners 1994–95.

Heavy Woollen Challenge Cup: Winners 1985–86, 1986–87 ('A' team)

Under–21 Rose Bowl: Winners 1950–51, 1951–52.

Under–19 League Cup: Winners 1949–50, 1951–52, 1952–53, 1953–54, 1956–57, 1957–58, 1958–59, 1950–60, 1960–61, 1962–63, 10963–64, 1964–65, 1965–66, 1966–67, 1967–68, 1968–69, 1969–70.

Under–19 Reporter Cup: Winners 1952–53, 1953–54, 1956–57, 1957–58, 1958–59, 1960–61, 1961–62, 1962–63, 1963–64, 1964–65, 1966–67, 1967–68, 1968–69, 1969–70, 1972–73.

Under–17 Oldroyd Trophy: Winners 1952–53, 1953–54, 1955–56, 1956–57, 1957–58, 1961–62, 1964–65, 1965–66, 1966–67, 1967–68, 1969–70, 1971–72.

Under–17 Boffin Trophy: Winners 1961-62, 1964-65, 1965-66, 1966-67, 1967-68, 1969–70.

Under–17 Trophy: Winners 1983–84, 1987–88.

Under–11 Heavy Woollen Cup: 1968–69, 1994–95.

Leeds & District Amateur Rugby League

Under–19 Continuation Cup: Winners 1966–67.

Under–17 Cup: Winners 1971–72.

Under–16 Cup: Winners 2016

Under–14 Cup: Winners 2017

Yorkshire Association of Boys Club (Rugby League competitions)

Rawson Cup: Winners 1954–55, 1956–57, 1959–60, 1961–62.

Bartlett Cup: Winners 1956–57, 1959–60, 1961–62.

Inter-County Seven-a-side

Sports Centre Trophy: Winners 1966.

Yorkshire County

Under—19 Cup: Winners 1963–64, 1971–72.

Under—17 Cup: 1969–70

Yorkshire League (Open Age)

Senior Division: Winners 1987–88, 1988–89.

Divisional League: Champions 1985–86.

Division Three: Winners 1986–87 (Open age 'A' team)

Under—19 Challenge Cup: Winners 1985–86.

Yorkshire Youth Championship (Under —17): Winners 1987–88.

Mermaid Trophy: Winners 1987–88

Kirklees Junior League

Under—15 League Cup: Winners 1974–75, 1976–77.

Sharks Open Age (Summer): Rugby League Conference Yorkshire Region Minor Premiership winners 2010.

Open Age 'A' team: John Kane Cup winners 2008, 2017

Yorkshire League:

Under—17s: Play-off champions 2007, 2008.

Under—17s: League Cup winners 2008

Under—15s: Continuation Cup winners 2008

Under—15s: League Champions, Yorkshire Cup and Challenge Cup winners 2010.

Under—14s: Continuation Cup winners 2007

Under—14s: Premier Division Champions 2007.

Under-13s: League Champions and Cup winners

Under—12s: League and Cup winners 2007

Co-operative Rugby League Conference Regional

Season	P	W	D	L	F	A	Pts	Place
2010	14	12	0	2	550	223	24	1
2011	10	6	2	2	280	262	14	3

National Conference League

Season	Division	P	W	D	L	F	A	Pts	Place
2011	Two	22	7	1	14	362	547	15	9/12
2012 Interim	Group G	10	3	0	7	176	385	6	3/4
2012	Two	24	17	1	6	568	382	35	4/13
2013	Two	18	15	0	3	539	306	30	2/10
2014	One	22	11	1	10	569	505	23	4/12
2015	One	26	15	1	10	726	524	31	4/14
2016	One	26	10	1	15	565	633	21	10/14

NB The top tier of the Conference is the Premier Division.

These records are not complete, and we apologise to any team whose achievements are not included.

Other books from London League Publications Ltd:

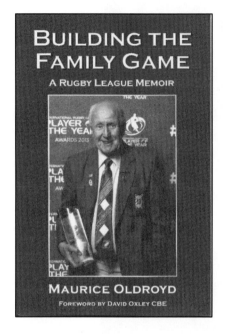

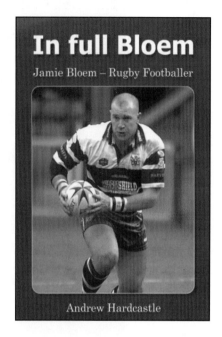

Maurice Oldroyd was one of the key people involved in the development of amateur rugby league since the foundation of the British Amateur Rugby League Association (BARLA) in 1973.

He was the Association's first full-time employee, and played a major role in its development until his retirement in 2000. However, he then became the Association's chairman from 2001 to 2005, and today is the Association's patron.

This fascinating memoir reflects on his life and involvement in rugby league. Maurice Oldroyd has been at the centre of amateur rugby league since 1973. This well- illustrated, fascinating memoir is essential reading for all rugby league fans. Published at £12.95, available for **just £5.00 post free in the UK** from www.llpshop.co.uk or by post from London League Publications Ltd, PO Box 65784, London NW2 9NS.

In full Bloem: The explosive biography of South African rugby league star Jamie Bloem, current referee and former Castleford, Oldham, Halifax, Widnes, Doncaster and Huddersfield player. He also played regularly for South Africa, and was capped by Scotland.

Published in February 2013 @ £14.95 (hardback), **just £6.95 post free in the UK** direct from London League Publications Ltd.

All our books can be ordered from any bookshop @ full price. To order direct from London League Publications Ltd visit our website: www.llpshop.co.uk or write to LLP, PO Box 65784, London NW2 9NS (cheques payable to London League Publications Ltd). Most of our books are available as E-Books for Kindle from Amazon.

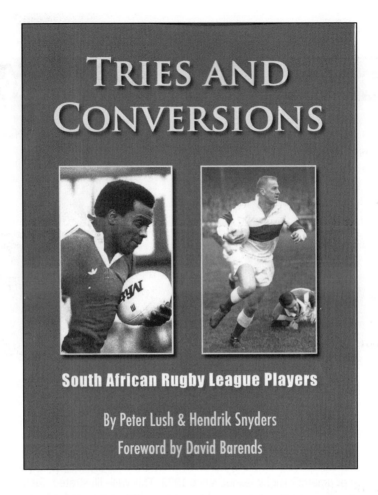

TRIES AND CONVERSIONS

South African Rugby League Players

By Peter Lush & Hendrik Snyders

Foreword by David Barends

In 1910, James Megson and William Mart became the first native-born South Africans to sign for British rugby league clubs. Since then, South African players have made a significant contribution to rugby league. This book is the first comprehensive study of their contribution to rugby league. It covers players who played in Great Britain and Australia. Some were very successful, such as Attie van Heerden and George van Rooyen in the 1920s, Tom van Vollenhoven, Alan Skene, Jan Prinsloo and Len Killeen in the 1950s and 1960s, and Mark Johnson and Jamie Bloem in the Super League era. But there were also players who never made it after switching codes to play rugby league, and their stories are also told here.

Available for just £13.95 post free in the UK direct from London League Publications Ltd or from Amazon.co.uk . Credit card orders via www.llpshop.co.uk; payment by cheque to PO Box 65784, London NW2 9NS. Available in bookshops at £14.95.
Also available as an E-Book for Kindle from Amazon.

Sully's Way
Mick Sullivan
Rugby League Legend
by Graham Williams

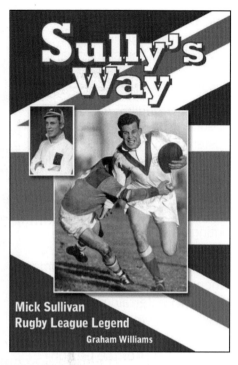

Mick Sullivan started playing rugby league at Shaw Cross. He was one of the greatest rugby league players of the post war period. He made a record 46 appearances for Great Britain in test matches, which was subsequently equalled by Garry Schofield. He also scored a record 41 test match tries. These records will probably never be beaten. He played in three World Cups, and was twice a World Cup winner, in 1954 and 1960.

He also had a successful career in club rugby league. He was a Challenge Cup winner three times, and played for **Huddersfield, Wigan, St Helens, York and Dewsbury.** He also played regularly for Yorkshire, and was a player-coach in Australia.

He was twice transferred for a world record fee – from Huddersfield to Wigan, and then from Wigan to St Helens. In 2013, he was made a member of the Rugby League Hall of Fame.

This authorised biography, which includes an introduction by his daughter Michelle, and forewords by Billy Boston and Danny Lockwood, covers his full career and life outside rugby league.

Published in September 2015. Available for just **£12.50 post free in the UK** direct from London League Publications Ltd or from Amazon.co.uk . Credit card orders via www.llpshop.co.uk; payment by cheque to PO Box 65784, London NW2 9NS. Available in bookshops at £12.95.
Also available as an E-Book for Kindle from Amazon.
Book details: 176 page paperback illustrated with photos.

The Glory and the Dream is a great new rugby league novel. It tells the story of a young boy's rite of passage. It is full of rich characters, and is played out against a backdrop of social upheaval in the austere post-war years of rationing and shortages. But it was a time when communities pulled together. Walking days, royal visits, Sunday School outings to the seaside and communal bonfire nights were annual highlights. It was a time when youngsters had to make their own entertainment, including playing rugby league. It is about Johnny Gregson, the young star of the Garton rugby league team, whose dream is to follow his dad's success in the sport. Johnny lives with his mother in Four Locks, a poor working class

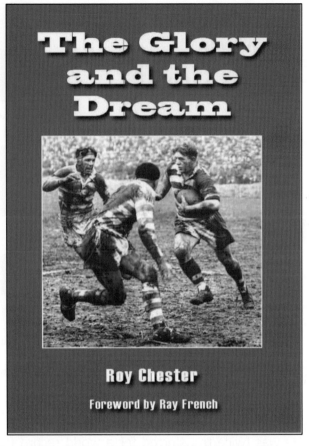

area in a grimy northern town. His father died in the Second World War. The story starts in 1945, when Johnny is aged 10. It follows his rise from junior rugby league through playing rugby union as a schoolboy to turning professional with Garton.

Johnny faces challenges at every turn, including when he wins a scholarship to a local public school and is labelled as a 'slum kid;' by the class bully. His prowess at rugby helps him deal with this boy. Also, at the tender age of 16, he meets a young woman who becomes very important to him. This is a story about sport, romance and working class life. It includes many humorous incidents, insights and even tragedy in a young man's development.

Published in March 2014 at £9.95. Order for **just £5.00 post free in the UK** from www.llpshop.co.uk or from London League Publications Ltd, PO Box 65784, London NW2 9NS. Also available on Amazon.co.uk

Also available as an E-Book for Kindle from Amazon.

70 YEARS
OF REACHING FORWARD
SHAW CROSS RUGBY LEAGUE CLUB

In 1947, a few youngsters from Shaw Cross wanted to play rugby league. They set up a team in Shaw Cross, which celebrated its 70th anniversary in 2017. During this time it has focused mainly on young people playing the game, although the first team now play in the National Conference League. Many famous players started their careers with Shaw Cross, including Mick Sullivan and Mike 'Stevo' Stephenson. The club has also done pioneering work through its international tours, including a longstanding link with French rugby league.

This remarkable story is told here. It includes:

- The club's early years
- Moving to Open Age rugby league
- International links and tours
- Playing in the Challenge Cup
- The club's Hall of Fame

Every rugby league fan will find this book of interest. It is a genuine grassroots sports story.

LONDON LEAGUE PUBLICATIONS LTD
£9.95 net in the United Kingdom

ISBN 978-1-909885-14-1